# ETHICS IN CONTEXT

# Ethics in Context

## Towards the Definition and Differentiation of the Morally Good

HOWARD P. KAINZ

*Professor of Philosophy*
*Marquette University, Milwaukee*

Foreword by Vernon J. Bourke

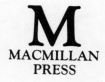

MACMILLAN
PRESS

First published 1988

Published by
THE MACMILLAN PRESS LTD
Houndmills, Basingstoke, Hampshire RG21 2XS
and London
Companies and representatives
throughout the world

Typeset by Wessex Typesetters
(Division of The Eastern Press Ltd)
Frome, Somerset

Printed in Hong Kong

British Library Cataloguing in Publication Data
Kainz, Howard P.
Ethics in context: towards the definition
and differentiation of the morally good.
1. Ethics—History
I. Title
170'.9          BJ71
ISBN 0–333–43611–3 (hc)
ISBN 0–333–43612–1 (pbk)

# Contents

v

*Contents*

# Foreword

## Vernon J. Bourke

While Howard Kainz in this book frankly asserts his debts to Aristotelian ethics and the Christian interpretation of Aristotle provided by Thomas Aquinas, his aim is not to return to Greek classicism or medieval scholasticism. Kainz sees ethics in the new context of present-day thinking, both Continental-European and British-American.

Much of his initial discussions are devoted to the comparison and differentiation of the aesthetic and moral good. But also involved is the question of whether ethical judgement rests on prior dispositions of the agent (good will, sense of duty, etc.) or on external and utilitarian considerations. All of this is reminiscent of Aristotle's notion that human well-being (*eudaimonia*) requires both activity in accord with virtue (an intra-psychic base) and some external advantages, such as good friends, health, good fortune (extra-psychic and objective). Here Kainz's readiness to see both sides of an issue prepares the way for a viable resolution of the problem.

Most people have not thought about what constitutes a really good life. Nor do they know how to go about the reasoning that might lead to an ideal of success as humans. Of course, many of us are so concerned about earning a living that we find little time to apply ourselves to philosophical questions. But what is more practical than considering how to live well? What is the point to having a mind, if we fail to use it on the most challenging of questions?

Not only students but also the general public should be interested in what it means to be a good person. In the literature of the history of ethics one may find dozens of answers to this problem. That is part of the difficulty: perhaps there are too many solutions. But that observation misses the point. In working out one's own philosophy of life (something no one else can do for you) it may be just as useful to study a bad solution (so that it may be quickly discarded) as to pursue a promising view (so that it may be developed and adapted to one's own circumstances).

That is what the present book can provide: much guidance from great minds of the past and present about the ideally good life. But a mere collection of such teachings might produce nothing but intellectual indigestion, so Howard Kainz offers his own evaluation of these many ethical stances. He further provides a good example of a thoughtful ethicist in action. He does not attempt to force you into his pattern of thought. But on the other hand he is convinced, and hopes you will be eventually subject to conviction, that some approaches to the notion of human well-being are definitely superior to others. Of course, we should not expect to find in ethics books the ready-made answers to our own moral problems. What they can offer is some help to people who are willing to do their own thinking.

In a court of law one test of whether the accused is responsible for his alleged offence is to enquire whether this person is able to distinguish good from bad action, right from wrong. Some wag has suggested that some present-day ethicists would have a difficult time with this test. Early in this century G. E. Moore startled the academic world when he wrote that, 'if it is not the case that "good" denotes something simple and indefinable, only two alternatives are possible: either it is a complex, a given whole, about the correct analysis of which there may be disagreement; or else it means nothing at all, and there is no such subject as Ethics' (Moore, *Principia Ethica*, ch. 1, sect. 13). Indeed, it is the case that a student, or any intelligent reader who is interested in a 'correct analysis' and is not completely satisfied with Moore's solution – intuitionism – may only be confused by extensive and unguided readings.

That is why a book such as *Ethics in Context* is a welcome contribution. It does not deny the difficulties inherent in the attempt to appraise what is good in human behaviour but it confronts the problem honestly and intelligently.

VERNON J. BOURKE
*Emeritus Professor of Philosophy*
*St Louis University*

# Preface

In the Introduction to my *Ethica Dialectica* (1979), I expressed some allegiance to an Aristotelian methodology – using dialectic as a prelude or propaedeutic to *episteme* or 'science', that is, a deductively organised, systematic presentation. In the works of Aristotle himself, the dialectical approach largely takes the form of a methodical sifting of past and current positions on an issue, before presenting scientific/systematic arguments for his own position. This approach was adopted with great success by Thomas Aquinas in the golden days of medieval scholasticism, but modern Thomists have largely abandoned the practice of systematically sifting *contemporary* positions in search of an acceptable 'middle' position. In the USA at present the closest approximation to the original Aristotelian–Thomistic approach is to be found in some of the projects and publications of Mortimer Adler's Institute for Philosophical Research, which has no explicit ties with Catholic philosophy and only very loose ties with Thomism.

In any case, the entirety of that earlier book may be taken as variations, extensions and expansions, on several levels, of the Aristotelian idea of dialectic. On the first level of dialectical opposition in *Ethica Dialectica*, the two opposed characters, Cranston and Turner, personified some of the standard contemporary oppositions of 'schools' in ethics – deontology *vs* teleology, idealism *vs* empiricism, synthesis *vs* analysis. On a second level of opposition, the topics they discussed were in the form of polarities – good and evil, 'ought' and 'is', subjective and objective moral standards, and so on. And on a third level of opposition, one might also observe that the two characters, to whom I tried to give equal weight, would oscillate between the convergence and the divergence of their own respective positions with those of the other. Attempts were made in various places, and especially in the Epilogue, to arrive at a synthetic formulation or tentative compromise. But the book as a whole did not get beyond the stage of dialectic. Thus its aim was not primarily to come up with definitive or even satisfactory answers to questions such as: 'how is "ought" derived from "is"?', 'what is meant by moral good?' or 'are there objective moral norms?' The primary aim was to lay out in full view some of the major opposing positions prevailing in ethics up to the present, and in necessarily artificial 'laboratory' fashion put them into proximity and interaction with one another, to see what modifications or further developments might be needed to enhance viability. And so, in Wittgensteinian terminology, the 'general form of the proposition' for that book was: 'such-and-such are some of the primary forms of ethical opposition'.

In contrast, the 'general form of the proposition' for the present book would be: 'such-and-such is the unity emerging out of the oppositions'. For this is a more systematic endeavour, beginning with the Aristotelian concept of ethics, in which the good, happiness, politics, and morality were interfused; and tracing out in systematic fashion some notable distinctions and ramifications that have emerged in the history of philosophy, without losing sight of Aristotle's original, synthetic insight. My approach departs somewhat from the specialised focus of the Anglo-American tradition in ethics, and is more in the continental tradition of the 'philosophy of law', in which, as D. D. Raphael notes, ethics is expressly considered in relation to other spheres, such as politics and law.[1] A classical example of this approach would be G. W. F. Hegel's *Philosophy of Right*, which begins with concepts of morality and law, and situates them gradually in the context of politics, international relations and history. Endeavouring in a similar way to situate ethics in its axiological context, I shall be concerned with defining the good in terms of its essential subjective/objective dynamisms; showing the relationship of the moral good to aesthetic and religious good, and the 'common good'; and finally, showing some of the contemporary interconnections between these spheres and some of the confusions that occasionally result from indiscriminate connections.

The contemporary analytic tradition in English and American philosophy has been largely concerned with meta-ethical questions; for example, questions about the meaning of ethical statements such as '$x$ is right'. If meta-ethical enquiry is carried too far, however, we find ourself in the position of the person who wants to learn to swim before jumping in the water, to use a Hegelian simile.[2] In other words, if we resolutely insist on solving questions such as 'what does "$x$ is right" mean?' before we give any serious attention to normative ethical questions, we keep ourselves from ever deciding whether $x$ is, indeed, right. For the tentative answers we come up with have a way of preventing all further meaningful enquiry, normative as well as meta-ethical. If, like A. J. Ayer, we interpret '*x* is right' emotivistically to mean 'hooray for *x*!', we are not only prevented from taking seriously any questions about right and wrong, but also are even prevented from taking Ayer's meta-ethical position seriously, because Ayer's 'my theory is right' becomes easily interpreted (according to a similar interpretative principle) as 'hooray for my theory!'. If, like some relativists, we interpret '*x* is right' to mean '*x* is favoured and enforced by society at large', we not only keep ourselves from taking seriously any rightness of actions not approved by society, but we leave ourselves open to a meta-interpretation, such that the statement 'my theory of relativism is right' is taken to mean 'my theory is acceptable to society (but not necessarily intrinsically right)'. If a naturalist were to assert categorically that '*x* is right' is always based on some natural experience relative to *x*, we would, if we took the naturalist seriously, be prevented from investigating the rightness of actions whose experiential bases are unknowable or unknown; but we might also object that the naturalist's meta-ethical statement is based on his or her experience, not on our own. And if we believe the intuitionist when he or she tells us that '*x* is right' simply reduces to 'I have immediate and inexplicable knowledge of the rightness of *x*', we would not only be prevented from ever speaking of the rightness of something concerning which people's intuitions differ, but also may object that we intuitively find intuitionism itself to be wrong when applied to first-order ethical decisions.

This is not meant to serve as a thoroughgoing refutation of meta-ethics, but simply to illustrate some of the impasses one could get into by carrying the re-interpretation of language – ethical or meta-ethical – to an extreme, and also to indicate why the focus of the systematic analysis conducted here will be more normative (that is, concerned with right behaviour) than meta-ethical (that is, concerned with the meaning of 'right', 'good', etc.).[3] As we proceed we shall discuss (in Chapter 2) the 'aesthetic/moral' sphere, in the limited context of which the meta-ethical claims discussed in the preceding paragraph seem to have normative significance and to be valid: for example, the 'moral sense' theory in its appropriate aesthetic/moral dimensions is a valid and reasonable form of intuitionism; theories of temperament give empirical evidence of the sort of situations in which specific emotivist interpretations are most valid; 'aesthetic/moral relativism', by avoiding the broad generalisations of meta-ethical relativism, promotes its own credibility; and contemporary theories such as sociobiology and Kohlberg's theory of moral development, if they restrict themselves to some modest claims about certain natural causes which have an effect on moral behaviour, focus our attention on that particular area in which naturalistic presuppositions seem to be most relevant. I might also add that what I have called the 'aesthetic/moral' sphere, as a whole, is a sphere in which meta-ethical hedonism, which has received an unnecessarily bad name, has a limited but significant and valid normative expression.

In Chapter 3 I consider a series of traditional classical theories in ethics which, while avoiding the extreme meta-ethical subjectivism which reduces all moral norms to subjective whims, nevertheless highlight the absolute importance of the subjective element in morality. This is followed by another series of positions which, while avoiding an extreme of meta-ethical objectivism which looks upon moral norms as positive laws, variously enforced, nevertheless argues for the existence and validity of certain objective norms for all human beings.

In sum, the problems connected with some meta-ethical positions seem to emerge if and when their claims and implications are extended in blanket fashion to all moral behaviour; whereas, if they are taken in a more limited, moderate, modest fashion within the parameters of certain spheres of aesthetics and normative ethics, they are indisputably valid.

Finally, amidst all the debates, normative and meta-ethical, going on in ethics, it is easily possible to lose sight completely of the idea of *moral good*, which presumably had given rise to the debates in the first place. The ultimate objective of this book, with which the final chapters are particularly concerned, is to rise temporarily above the historical positions and systematic arguments to show how the idea of moral good can be satisfactorily differentiated, reappropriated, retained and accentuated. Since my interpretation of moral good in Chapter 5 is not based on linguistic analysis, perhaps it will not be susceptible to any facile rebuttal on linguistic grounds. However, in view of the past history of ethics, it would be temerarious to claim that any ethical interpretation or position is irrefutable.

As will become obvious to my readers, this book is primarily an attempt at synthesis. It is based on the optimistic judgement that the vast number of approaches in classical and modern ethics, far from being a Macbethian 'tale told by an idiot full of sound and fury, signifying nothing', have evinced patterns of order and organisation among themselves, in spite of the perennial individualistic antipathy of philosophers to explicitly collaborative efforts.

I should like to thank Professors Vernon Bourke and Henry Veatch and my colleagues Michael Wreen, Eileen Sweeney and Richard Davis for kindly consenting to offer their comments and criticisms on the various versions of this book. If I have not been able to address successfully some of their criticisms even in this final version, this, of course, is no reflection on them. Also, I am indebted to Barbara Babcock, Mary Glazewski and Grace Jablonski for typing the various versions of the manuscript; to Brad Wronski, Bob Abele and Maureen Milligan for assistance with research and proof-reading; and to Marquette University for some released time and grants to offset the costs of research and writing.

# 1

# Aristotelian 'Happiness', Revisited

## ARGUMENT

*The history of systematic ethics in Western philosophy begins with Aristotle, who in his immensely influential* Nicomachean Ethics *sought to characterise ethical activity in terms of, of all things, 'happiness' – very broadly defined, and with an emphasis on a very objective state of affairs rather than on subjective experiences. Does the Aristotelian approach and definition, which shows very little cognizance of what in the contemporary world are called 'moral intentions' and 'moral problems', still have any significance for us, and for the Kantians, utilitarians and others whose theories are most prominent now, and whose approach and concerns seem to be very different from those of Aristotle?*

Aristotle's *Nicomachean Ethics*, the first major systematic treatise in ethics in the history of Western philosophy, begins with the pursuit of happiness as the self-evident goal of moral thinking. If it sounds strange, or at least a bit artificial or forced, to our modern ears to hear that *morality* is in some way necessarily connected with *happiness*, perhaps that strangeness itself should be an extra incentive to reinvestigate Aristotle's starting point, to see whether he might not have been misled himself, thus setting Western ethics off, so to speak, on the wrong foot; or whether perhaps our own notions of happiness, morality, or the good might need some constructive modifications.

Let us begin with Aristotle's initial and broad definition of happiness (*Eudaimonia*):

Human good [happiness] turns out to be activity of soul in accordance with virtue, and if there is more than one virtue, [it is]

1

in accordance with the best and most complete. But we must add 'in a complete life'. For one swallow does not make a summer, nor does one day. . . . Yet evidently happiness needs the external goods as well. . . . For the man who is very ugly in appearance or ill-born or solitary and childless is not very likely to be happy, and perhaps a man would be still less likely if he had thoroughly bad children or friends or had lost good children or friends by death. . . . Why then should we not say that he is happy who (1) is active in accordance with complete virtue and (2) is sufficiently equipped with external goods, not for some chance period but throughout a complete life?[1]

This definition would probably strike a responsive chord in most members of Western industrialised society, although modifications would have to be made for singles and some two-career couples, and aspiration levels would have to be somewhat lower for the ugly, handicapped, abjectly poor, oppressed, etc. But the depiction is close enough to the idea most people have of happiness; so that we may take it as a starting point. And as we subject it to further analysis, we begin to notice, first of all, that it lends itself (a) 'latitudinally' to a differentiation of aesthetic and strictly ethical levels or dimensions; and (b) 'longitudinally' to a certain subjective/ objective polarity. The intersection of 'latitudinal' and 'longitudinal' aspects can be diagrammatically illustrated (see Figure 1).

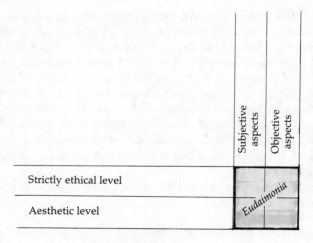

**Figure 1**

## 1(a)  THE AESTHETIC/MORAL DIMENSIONS

The depiction that Aristotle gives of happiness is by no means a 'still life' portrayal. Although a certain amount of passive possession and enjoyment of one's surroundings is indicated, movement is introduced into these surroundings when Aristotle speaks of 'activity of the soul according to virtue'. But the two things, the aesthetic enjoyment and the virtuous activity are conjoined, existing side by side, perhaps a bit too close together. And it is for this reason that the existentialist, Søren Kierkegaard, criticised Aristotle for expounding an 'aesthetic' ethics, in which virtue is not enough, but must be propped up with all manner of aesthetic diversions.[2] But Kierkegaard on his part reacted perhaps too strongly to Aristotle's initial characterisation of happiness. As we proceed further in the *Nicomachean Ethics*[3] it becomes clear that 'activity according to (moral and intellectual) virtue' is not just an ingredient contributing to the total effect of a happy life, but the *sine qua non*. If, for example, our Athenian citizen had health, beauty, family, friends, prosperity and a long life without virtuous activity, he would not be happy; and if, on the other hand, there were another citizen who had the virtue but barely enough of the above-mentioned concomitants he would be essentially happy, although lacking a full aesthetic complement to enhance his life.

In any depiction of happiness or the good, there is an important distinction to be made between the aesthetic and the ethical dimensions, which are often confused. An extreme case may help to highlight the distinction: consider an archetypal playboy who 'has everything' – money from a massive inheritance, health, physical attractiveness, love, friends, unlimited consumer goods and freedom of movement – and who is totally involved in going from one enjoyment to another. The *prima facie* profile is one of unmitigated happiness. But we do not have to be extreme moralists to realise, with a modicum of reflection, that the reality may be very different. The potential for unhappiness, in a life like this, derives from the fact that the style of life is inimical to personal development, to the efforts involved in self-determination and successful creative accomplishment, and to the experience of self-worth. An individual in such circumstances, if he makes any progress in self-consciousness, may find himself wondering one day: What have I ever accomplished on my own? How is the world better for my existence? How can I be sure that any of my friends like me for what I am, rather than for what I can give them?

Contrasted with this extreme, is another extreme, with which we are also familiar: the individual who is willing to sacrifice many of the 'aesthetic' dimensions of the good life – wealth, prestige, etc. – in order to find 'happiness' in a simpler, more harmonious existence; an existence that Aristotle would call 'virtuous' in so far as it involved a maximum activation of man's highest faculties, the specifically human faculties of practical and theoretical reason.

But happiness, or the good, to be *complete* requires both – a certain minimum of aesthetic enjoyment as well as the virtuous activity specific to man.

## 1(b)  SUBJECTIVE/OBJECTIVE POLARITY

Aristotle, reacting rather strongly to Plato's doctrine that all good, even human good, was a transcendent 'Idea' subsisting in some extramundane realm, was intent on showing how the idea of the good was devised from our experience of *this* world, and in particular on showing how 'the good' for man, the goal to which he is directed by nature, is equivalent to what we call 'happiness'. But 'happiness' is not an altogether satisfactory translation of *eudaimonia*, the term used by Aristotle, which connoted to the Greeks primarily *good fortune* (including external prosperity), and secondarily a subjective state of well-being. The corresponding English term is similarly ambivalent; it is used to designate a state of *subjective contentment*, but it can also be used to convey a state of good fortune and security, as in the first psalm of the Old Testament, which begins: 'Happy the man who does not enter into the counsels of the wicked.' The obsolete English word, 'weal' (as in 'commonweal'), would be a closer approximation to *eudaimonia*.

In any case, the ambiguity which is built into the term corresponds quite appropriately to a certain bipolarity in the *idea* of 'happiness' itself. In the impressive picture of the happy Athenian citizen that Aristotle provides us with, we can make a rather clear-cut mental distinction between (a) the subjective experience of happiness, resulting from the appropriate physical and mental dispositions and reactions; and (b) the indispensable objective correlates of happiness – the external goods, the friends, the types of activity our Athenian engages in, and perhaps also that which he accomplishes or produces.

Complete happiness of the sort that Aristotle conceptualised would require a co-ordination of the two aspects, subjective and objective. There is admittedly an emphasis in Aristotle on what we might call the 'externals' of happiness, but he also clearly makes the point that if our virtuous and comfortable Athenian citizen were not *enjoying* his virtue, an important aspect would be missing.[4] And we moderns, convinced of the importance of the 'principle of subjectivity', might want to emphasise that aspect even more strongly than Aristotle.

The necessary co-ordination of the subjective and objective aspects of happiness might be illustrated by an analogy with Plato's ancient theory of perception.[5] Plato characterised perception as a result of the meeting of effusions coming from a sense organ and from a suitable object, for example, the perception of colour resulting from the meeting or marriage of effusions from the eye and from the coloured object, respectively. So also, we may say that for happiness there must be a conjunction of (a) certain subjective dispositions, and (b) some suitably gratifying objects or objectives. As applied to the 'aesthetic' dimension of happiness, this would imply a conjunction of (a) the proper physical and mental capacities and dispositions, with (b) congruent aesthetic objects or objectives. As applied to the 'ethical' dimension, the conjunction in question would be more specifically of (a) the proper attitudes, dispositions, and habits of the soul, with (b) unimpeded, harmonious, virtuous, and, to some extent, successful, activity.

To sum up, if we follow Aristotle in trying to define the good on the basis of our ordinary experience in this world, we end up with the experience of happiness itself, which can be distinguished into aesthetic and ethical dimensions, each of which dimensions manifests a certain polarity or dialectic of subjective and objective aspects.

Before we go on to consider the aesthetic and ethical dimensions in greater detail, we should take note by way of anticipation of an important discrepancy which will become explicit later between the Aristotelian conception of happiness and the good, and the way that some major modern ethicists, Kant and the utilitarians being particularly salient examples, have conceptualised happiness and the good.

## 1(c)  KANTIAN 'HAPPINESS' AND UTILITARIAN 'GOOD'

Kant in his ethical works concentrates exclusively on what we have designated the 'aesthetic' aspects of happiness. 'Happiness' is defined by him as 'the entire satisfaction of wants and inclinations'.[6] In some places,[7] he raises the question whether virtuous or dutiful activity is not itself a kind of satisfaction, which could be taken as an incentive to morality – and he dismisses this idea peremptorily. Kant's theory is still one of the most influential ethical theories in contemporary Western philosophy, and we shall consider it, as well as utilitarianism, in greater detail in Chapter 3. But for the present, we should simply note some initial contrasts between the Aristotelian and the more recent theories.

Offhand, it would seem that a theory such as Aristotle's, which extolled virtuous activity as the principle of happiness, must propound an idea of 'virtue' sharply different from a theory such as Kant's, which sees in man's life on earth no *necessary* connection at all between virtuous activity and happiness.[8] How could Kant's theory be *attractive*? Or are we to suppose that there is some higher level of attractiveness which does not qualify as 'happiness'? The discrepancy seems to result from the fact that the Kantian theory portrays happiness as much more passive than does Aristotle's, and also, although it presents a very lofty view of human nature, seems to relegate 'happiness' to the lower, that is, the sensory functions of human nature. The net effect of this interpretation is to *sever the moral good from happiness*.

The utilitarians, on the other hand, although they agree with Aristotle that morality is necessarily connected with the pursuit of the good or happiness, specifically limit the scope of the good to 'non-moral' good. According to utilitarianism, one does not become moral by intentionally pursuing specifically *moral* good. But strangely enough, by intentionally pursuing a-moral or non-moral good (that is, happiness) for themselves and others, the utilitarians presumably become morally good!

Although utilitarians diverge sharply from Kant in their greater willingness to connect moral good with 'happiness' (non-moral good), both utilitarians and Kantians find themselves in agreement in one important respect: *moral* good is not necessarily in any important way related to the actual *causation* of happiness.

Such a belief (that our happiness is not in any way dependent on morality) may seem strange and, if widely subscribed to, may even be seen to portend some unfortunate social and cultural consequences! But it may also be understood as a natural 'equal and opposite reaction' to the fusion of the aesthetic and the ethical in Aristotle's initial and influential formulation. To avoid, if possible, the necessity for such a reaction, I will endeavour in the next chapter to differentiate the aesthetic from the moral. This strategem should help disencumber my subsequent discussion of the moral from 'excess baggage' and pave the way at a minimum for the conclusion that morality in some way contributes to happiness in some very important sense.

# 2

# Aesthetic Good

## ARGUMENT

*In our day, we tend to equate morality with duty and obligation, which often runs contrary to our desires or dispositions. So it sounds strange to our modern ears to hear Aristotle portraying the moral life as involving friendship, a happy family life, beauty, wealth, luck, proper psychological dispositions, health and fulfilling activities. A modern moralist might object, 'what do these things have to do with morality?' In actual fact, however, a great deal, perhaps even the greater part, of our 'moral life' is closely intertwined with such 'aesthetic' aspects. In the following chapter we examine that intermediary area of aesthetic/moral behaviour. This analysis will focus on (1) the subjective dispositions conducive to aesthetic/moral behaviour, and (2) objective biological, psychological and social facts which are conducive to aesthetic/moral behaviour or ideas concerning it.*

## 2(a)  TERMINOLOGICAL CONSIDERATIONS

In contemporary parlance, 'aesthetic' is used to refer to the appreciation of beauty, particularly in conjunction with the fine arts. This usage is also prevalent in philosophy, a branch of which – 'aesthetics' – is often said to be concerned exclusively or at least primarily with the arts of 'high culture' – painting, sculpture, poetry, drama, classical music, ballet and opera. Some philosophers have seen this as overly and unnecessarily élitist. They view so-called 'lower' culture – for example, crafts, photography, architecture and jazz – as also worthy of serious aesthetic analysis. Arthur Biermann, for example, warns that art has now become the province of an economic and intellectual élite, who fail to realise that the traditional 'fine arts' are only a subclass, and sometimes a trivial subclass, of art.[1] Some would want to go even further and extend the interest and scope of aesthetics to the beauty of natural

8

phenomena as well as art.[2] Still others take exception to the restriction of aesthetics to the 'higher senses' (sight and hearing) and the appreciation of beauty in the strict sense, and opt for an expansion of the boundaries of aesthetics to objects of touch and taste, atmosphere, artificial implements, sports, etc.[3] It is interesting to note, however, that even in the latter 'liberal' group, very few have endeavoured to apply the concept of aesthetics to the area of interpersonal erotic/romantic attraction (although one wonders whether this is not the paradigmatic locus of aesthetic experience for most people, including the élitists).

While trying to maintain our own proper 'aesthetic distance' from such ongoing controversies, we will take our cue from the more liberal aestheticians and use the term 'aesthetic' here in the widest sense possible – to encompass not only the appreciation and creation of artistic works, but all enjoyable experiences and activities and their corresponding objects or objectives, including those comprised in Aristotle's aforementioned definition of happiness (friends, physical attractiveness, health, material goods, etc.). This extension of the applicability of 'aesthetics' also has some etymological grounding, in so far as the Greek *aisthetikos* simply means 'having to do with sensation or feeling'.

## 2(b)  METHODOLOGICAL CONSIDERATIONS

In meta-aesthetics (analysis of the various theories of aesthetics), a distinction is sometimes made between 'subjectivist' and 'objectivist' theories of aesthetics. The former are characterised as interpreting aesthetic values in terms of the attraction that gives rise to them, such that 'beauty is' quite literally 'in the eye of the beholder'. The latter are said to explain aesthetic values as conditioned by certain properties intrinsic to aesthetic objects, such as the qualities of unity, complexity and intensity (or character) that Monroe Beardsley designates as the 'canons' according to which aestheticity should be evaluated.[4] But neither of these polarised approaches seems to work well *in abstraction*.

If, for example, there were an object that had all three of Beardsley's 'canonical' properties, but which no one in the world ever felt any interest in, it could scarcely establish a strong claim to being aesthetic. If, on the other hand, everyone in the world had an uncontrollable, pathological attraction for some object which was disintegrating and alienating – for example, scenes of torture – we would still have some legitimate hesitation about granting that the experience in question was 'aesthetic' in the fullest sense. As Frederick Kainz observes,

> The extremes of subjectivism and objectivism are equally unacceptable solutions to the central problem of aesthetics. The question of whether the understanding and attitude of the perceiver or the objective characteristic of the object-of-concern is first in importance when beauty comes to be, is like the familiar, meaningless, but vexing question of whose act is more essential in the creating of a child, that of a man or that of a woman. Because both are absolutely necessary, neither partner can be foregone. In the same way with respect to aesthetic value one can only ask this question: since the proportion of the participation of subjective and objective factors can vary, what in a particular instance occurs because of the objective one and what because of that of attitude? An aesthetic value-experience comes into being only when a suitable object works on a receptive mind – that is, on one capable of and disposed towards the proper (adequate) psychic act.[5]

Some sort of interplay (in F. Kainz's terminology, 'correlativism') between subjective attraction and objective desirability seems to be in order. The two sides or aspects have to work in tandem to produce aesthetic values, and veridical aesthetic experience. And so, in analysing aesthetic good, and also, as we shall see, the other types of good, we will endeavour to focus on the subjective/objective dynamics of the experience, in order to maintain as much as possible a 'middle ground' between subjectivism and objectivism, or, to speak in more general metaphilosophical categories, between extremes of idealism and realism.

But, before we focus on subjective/objective dynamics, we should note, in order to avoid them, some equivocations prevalent in the use of the terms, 'subjective' and 'objective':

In *Philosophy and the Mirror of Nature*,[6] Richard Rorty, discussing the works of T. S. Kuhn, A. J. Ayer and others, points out some prevailing ambiguities in the use of 'subjective' and 'objective'. The following chart may bring to mind some usages and/or prejudices you may have been exposed to:

|              | 'Subjective'                                                                      |              | 'Objective'                                                              |
|--------------|-----------------------------------------------------------------------------------|--------------|--------------------------------------------------------------------------|
| (1) | a matter of taste | | capable of being settled by previously statable algorithm |
| (2) | incapable of eliciting universal rational agreement | | that about which there is general agreement among sane and rational persons |
| (3) | irrelevant to the subject-matter of some theory being considered by rational discussants | | agreed upon by rational discussants after thorough sifting of the evidence |
| (4) | just existing in the 'heart' or in some confused portion of the mind | | 'out there', existing in the real world |

Note that the various meanings of 'subjective' here show a rather weak face. Almost anyone would prefer to be aligned with the varieties of 'objectivity' arrayed in the right-hand column. One reason for this seems to be our admiration for the physical sciences, which are taken to be paragons of objectivity (ironically at a time when one of the 'hardest' of the sciences, quantum physics, has taken the lead in emphasising the importance and unavoidability of contributions made by the observing subject to the elaboration of the data relevant in microphysics).

In an earlier formulation,[7] I distinguished two main alternative senses of the objective/subjective antinomy: (a) 'objective' as a standard or indisputable criterion *vs* 'subjective' as capricious and individualistic; and (b) 'objective' as external and publicly observable as opposed to 'subjective' as hidden within the psyche. My alternative (a) runs parallel to the first three senses differentiated by Rorty above; while my alternative (b) is similar to Rorty's fourth sense, except that my description of the 'subjective' aspect is more neutral, less pejorative.

In any case, the sort of antitheses we have just pointed out are too sharp to accommodate adequately the more nuanced relationships and the subjective/objective interactions germane to aesthetic, moral and other kinds of good, where, aside from some extremes (which will be discussed), there is only a relative *emphasis* on the subjective or objective aspects, not a one-sided insistence on the one or the other. Thus, for example, as we shall see, Kant's moral philosophy emphasises a *subjective* 'testing' process to determine the truly *objective* moral norms; while utilitarianism emphasises the *objective* sort of consequences we should strive to create with our *subjective* calculations or deliberations. To accommodate the sometimes complex but, I believe, also very important, interactions of subjective and objective factors in the analyses which follow, I offer the following working definitions, which indicate relative emphases while maintaining neutrality (that is, not prejudging subjectivity as in some way inferior to objectivity): 'subjective' = originating within the psyche, but not necessarily arbitrary or capricious; 'objective' = in some way external to the individual psyche, although not unrelated to the intentions or abilities of the psyche.

## 2(c)   AESTHETIC GOOD PROPER

The S/O dynamics of aesthetic good can be schematised in the following manner, to indicate the range of possibilities:

| Subjective disposition | Correspondence to objective standards, formal or informal, derived from nature or society | Result |
|---|---|---|
| Attraction | Unattractive or minimally attractive | Little or no aesthetic good |
| No attraction or minimal attraction | Attractive | Little or no aesthetic good |
| Attraction | Attractive | Aesthetic good (enjoyment) |

Since aesthetic experiences demonstrate either an emphasis on passive experiences (for example, contemplating a beautiful object) or active experiences (for example, creating a beautiful object), we shall, in the chart that follows, offer some rather extreme examples of each type to illustrate the S/O dynamics obtaining in this pre-ethical sphere:

*Passive experiences*

| Subjective disposition (SD) | Objective correspondence (OC) | Result |
|---|---|---|
| Afficionado of rock music sees signs saying 'free concert this way', and follows the signs immediately with great expectations | The rock artists are amateurs, the music is out-dated, and the accoustics are terrible | Incomplete aesthetic good (AG) (deficient OC) |
| I haven't eaten for two days and am ravenously hungry | The only things available to eat are some edible, but tasteless, hard-to-digest and slightly toxic plants | Incomplete AG (deficient OC) |
| I have a murderous hangover after an ill-advised drinking bout | I am presented with my favourite menu – roast beef salad and ice-cream | Incomplete AG (deficient SD) |
| Don Juan (to introduce a variation into Mozart's *Don Giovanni*), having completed his 1003rd seduction, feels completely jaded, and wants to have no more to do with women | He suddenly comes upon the perfect woman, the woman he has always dreamed about. She can't understand why he seems to show no interest, and abruptly departs. | Incomplete AG (deficient SD) |
| Don Juan (to introduce a variation on the sub-play of George Bernard Shaw's *Man and Superman*) is released from hell after several hundred years, and looks forward breathlessly to meeting a woman, any woman | There has been a nuclear war, and the only woman remaining is Brunhild, the world's foremost man-hater, who prides herself on having personally cannibalised 1003 men | Incomplete AG (deficient OC) |
| George Armstrong, world's greatest football fan, comes down with kidney stones | As George is writhing in the X-ray room, the doctors and nurses watch George's favourite team win the final and decisive game | Incomplete AG (deficient SD) |

*Active Experiences*

| | | |
|---|---|---|
| Vladimir Sharokov, psychologically distraught after an argument with his wife, nevertheless has to give his scheduled ballet performance | The audience and critics, interested only in his unique style of dancing do not notice his lack of enthusiasm | Incomplete AG (deficient SD) |
| Vladimir Sharokov, on another occasion, is in superb form, ready to give a truly dazzling performance | His performance is in a foreign country in which the audience and critics find both his performance and the musical accompaniment uninteresting and largely unintelligible | Incomplete AG (deficient OC) |
| Andy Thompson, the famous newspaper columnist, has 'writer's block', and finds his daily writing assignments a form of torture | His reputation is secure, and the public still hangs on his every word | Incomplete AG (deficient SD) |
| Thompson gets a 'second wind', and starts writing easily again | His writing style becomes more literary than journalistic, and he loses his sense of what his readers are interested in. Even his devoted fans desert him | Incomplete AG (deficient OC) |

To generalise on the examples, aesthetic good – the strictly aesthetic dimension of happiness – requires a meshing of some minimal subjective attraction, motivation or interest with some minimal correspondence to written or unwritten prevailing objective norms, for aesthetic enjoyment to take place. In the overall context of our analysis of the good, our focus has been on the pre-moral dimensions of the good and happiness. We have concentrated on relatively clear-cut cases in which two *different* aesthetic orientations, or an aesthetic orientation and an *ethical* resolve, were *not* in conflict and have disregarded conceivable conflicts. For example, my active aesthetic participation in sports might conflict with my interest in music, or with my duties to my sick mother. Such considerations, which easily suggest themselves, would needlessly encumber our analysis, which is not intended to provide precise criteria for judging all cases.

We turn now to a consideration of an area which is still aesthetic, but often confused with the moral. Treated as an important but distinguishable dimension, it can supply a natural bridge to the area that may be designated more specifically moral.

## 2(d)   AESTHETIC/MORAL  GOOD

The moral sphere is concerned with behaviour. Can we maintain an aesthetic orientation in our moral behaviour? Certainly no one would want to contemplate leaving aesthetics completely behind, in most of his or her moral behaviour. And fortunately, it is not necessary to do so; for there is indeed a large area of human behaviour which is very much in line with our aesthetic orientations, and also converges with what is generally called 'moral' behaviour. Needless to say, the cultivation of this area is very important in the pursuit of happiness. We are all faced with multifarious expectations relating to our behaviour, and the 'safety valve' which helps us to avoid psychological pressure or emotional stress from these expectations is our ability at times to 'compromise' – to fulfil our inclinations at the same time as we conform to objective norms of behaviour.

A few examples will serve to illustrate the subjective/objective dynamisms in accord with the schema introduced earlier:

| Subjective disposition | Objective correspondence | Result |
|---|---|---|
| Roger is by nature very shy, sensitive to loud voices and finds it hard to deal with large groups of people | Because of his position in the company he works for, he is expected to sponsor occasional social functions. So he has a big party at his house | Incomplete aesthetic/moral good (deficient SD) |
| Sonja is very generous by nature, and enjoys doing things for people, especially her family | She happens to be in the town where her son is attending a university, so she meets him as he comes out of class and gives him a new shirt, a new watch and cash. Her son is visibly embarrassed, and he tells his friends he will see them later. She can't understand why her little surprise doesn't please him | Incomplete A/M good (deficient OC) |

| Subjective disposition | Objective correspondence | Result |
|---|---|---|
| I am throwing a party and feel very much opposed to admitting uninvited guests | My brother returns from China unexpectedly after a three-year absence, and appears at my door. I tell him to come back tomorrow | Incomplete A/M good (deficient OC) |
| An eighteen-year-old boy is anxious to help out with his educational expenses, and so takes on a part-time job | He has to be constantly told what to do. Otherwise, he spends his time idly | Incomplete A/M good (deficient OC) |
| A politician wants to get the vote of a particular town | He goes there, kisses the babies and visits the blue-collar workers, and hugs the mayor, even though he doesn't like babies and blue-collar workers, and detests the mayor of the town | Incomplete A/M good (deficient SD) |
| Martha is the active type, wants adventure and excitement, and the opportunity to visit new and mysterious places | She joins the navy, and is assigned to a base in a foreign country she always wanted to visit. | A/M good |

Clearly, the problematic in the Aesthetic/Moral area is finding, or learning to find, a linkage between personal interests, aptitudes, or personality traits and some modes of behaviour conforming suitably to existing objective norms. The search for such linkages is hampered by the vague and overly general idea we have of 'subjective dispositions' and 'conformity to objective norms'. Just what *are* these factors, more specifically? Some rather concerted attempts have been made in the history of philosophy and other disciplines to give greater specification to both factors:

## 2(d) 1.　Attempts to Clarify Aesthetic/Moral Subjective Dispositions

### 2(d) 1.1.　*Moral Sense Theories*
The 'common denominator' in moral sense theories is that they argue for some kind of special faculty, ability, or 'knack' of the human psyche which will (unless obstructed by external factors)

help man to make just the right moral decisions. A precursor of the moral sense theories is the cogitative power (*vis cogitativa*) hypothesised by Thomas Aquinas and other medieval scholastics, apparently as an interpretation of Aristotle's doctrine concerning the way that the mind relates to sensory particulars.[8] The cogitative power is described by Aquinas as something analogous to instinct (the *vis aestimativa*) in animals. Just as animals are equipped by nature with instincts which impel them to do certain things (build nests, weave webs, etc.) which are necessary for the perpetuation of their species, so also are all men similarly equipped with a special interior sense which enables them quasi-instinctively to make prudent judgements about contingent matters of choice in matters of behaviour.[9] Because of the existence of this power, the sensual appetites of men cannot really be compared with the amoral and arational appetites of the lower animals, but rather 'have a certain nobility, precisely insofar as they are so constituted as to be obedient to reason'.[10] The cogitative power thus brings it about that the human sense appetites often naturally, far from obstructing morality, co-operate in facilitating prudential, moral behaviour.

The idea of a kind of natural co-operation between sense appetites and reason also occurred to Anthony Ashley Cooper, the Earl of Shaftesbury (1671–1713), who coined the term 'moral sense' to describe a human faculty for combining aesthetic and moral judgement. The concept of a moral sense was adopted from Shaftesbury by the Scottish philosopher, Francis Hutcheson (1694–1746), in his books, *An Inquiry into the Original of our Ideas of Beauty and Virtue* (1725), and *An Essay on the Nature and Conduct of the Passions and Affections with Illustrations on the Moral Sense* (1728). The more widely influential Scottish philosopher, David Hume (1711–76) propounded a similar idea in his *Treatise of Human Nature* (1740). There are diverse interpretations and applications to be found in all these authors, but they seem to agree in holding for an innate human ability to bring about and maintain a harmony between sense appetites and reason, between aesthetics and morals. Hume's ethics in particular, with its explicit basis in the passions or 'sentiments', and with its rejection of rationalistic or *a priori* systems based on unreal and unnatural 'oughts', was a paradigmatic aesthetic/moral stance.

Some similarities to the moral sense theory are to be found in the German romantics, who shared with Hume *et al.* the ideal of bringing about a combination of the aesthetic and the moral.

Friedrich Schiller (1759–1805), for example, in his *Aesthetic Education of Man* (25th letter), writes,

> We must . . . be no longer at a loss to find a passage from sensuous dependence to moral freedom, after we have seen, in the case of Beauty, that the two [the sensuous and the moral] can perfectly well subsist together, and that in order to show himself spirit man does not need to eschew Matter.

A somewhat similar concept is to be found in *The Science of Ethics* of Johann Gottlieb Fichte (1762–1814), who held that, in matters of conscience, 'Whether I doubt, or am certain, is a matter which I become conscious of, not through argumentation . . . but through immediate feeling.'[11]

Some contemporary theories rely on presuppositions of a kind of moral intuition in the making of moral decisions.[12] Their principles bear some resemblances to moral sense theory; but the optimism of the moral sense theorists about combining the aesthetic *with* the moral is conspicuously lacking in twentieth century 'intuitionist' ethics.

### 2(d) 1.2. *Theories of Temperament*

The notion of a bedrock of feeling that will give impetus to morality through a 'moral sense' is, of course, rather vague. One wonders *what sort of* specific feelings and dispositions are related to moral behaviour, and *how* they are so related. The various theories of temperament, ancient and modern, actually endeavour to go into the specifics, to determine how individuals differ in regard to basic emotional or dispositional makeup, and even to make some connections between this basic makeup and certain types of value-orientation.

Temperament is defined by Sheldon as 'the level of personality just above physiological function and below acquired attitudes and beliefs. It is the level where basic patterns of motivation manifest themselves'.[13] Sheldon sees temperament as a kind of intermediate zone between the physical and the mental aspects of the human psyche, a natural endowment of impulses and orientations that one builds upon in becoming a definable personality. The psychologist Gordon Allport describes the nature of this original endowment in somewhat more detail:

Temperament refers to the characteristic phenomena of an individual's nature, including his susceptibility to emotional stimulation, his customary strength and speed of response, the quality of his prevailing mood, and all the peculiarities of fluctuation and intensity of mood, these being phenomena regarded as dependent on constitutional make-up, and therefore largely hereditary in origin.[14]

If temperament is indeed hereditary, it will provide us with an internal and potentially moral 'capital', a cluster of orientations differing from individual to individual, which may permit a more concrete explication of the very general notions of disposition, inclination, feeling, attraction, etc., with which we begin in an aesthetic ethics. Examples of how this explication takes place will be seen as we now offer a brief overview of some stages in the development of temperament theory.

A rough sketch of a theory of temperament was devised by the Greek physician Hippocrates (460–377 BC), who in his treatise *On Human Nature* differentiated four personality 'types' based on predominance of four hypothesised 'humours' in the body – black bile, yellow bile, blood and phlegm – leading to four corresponding temperament 'types', the melancholic, choleric, sanguine and phlegmatic temperaments. This theory seems to be presupposed by Aristotle in his analysis of various virtues and of the phenomenon of moral weakness, or incontinence in his ethics.[15] Another Greek physician, Galen (129–99 AD), elaborated the theory even further, and this elaborated theory, minus the emphasis on the 'humour' hypothesis, is taken for granted in the philosophical anthropology of some eighteenth- and nineteenth-century philosophers.[16] The personality traits commonly associated with the four types have entered into our language: the 'melancholic' person is one who is given to brooding, is overly suspicious and sensitive, and finds it difficult to maintain amicable social relations; the 'choleric' person is one who is hard-driving, irascible, highly active and self-directed; the 'sanguine' person is easygoing, changeable, highly social; and the 'phlegmatic' person is slow-moving and placid, but dependable. It was thought that most people would be intermediate between such extremes, but that to be strongly endowed with a certain temperament formation could affect one in some quasi-ethical respects. For example, the sanguine person would tend to be more generous and sympathetic than others, the choleric would tend to be more courageous and industrious. Some nineteenth-century physiologists vainly tried to give a modern physical underpinning to the four-temperament theory by basing it, for example, on interrelationships of hormones, or on neurological make-up. But some modest success has been achieved by twentieth-century psychologists, who have concentrated on the psychological rather than the physical factors, and have replaced the four independent and irreducible 'types' with two orthogonal dimensions, the dimension of emotionality and the dimension of changeability, as illustrated in Figure 2, which is based on Immanuel Kant's original descriptions of the traits, rearranged along lines originally suggested by the German psychologist, Wilhelm Wundt (1832–1920).

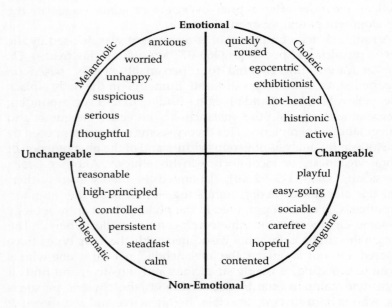

**Figure 2**
Diagram reprinted from H. J. Eysenck, *The Biological Basis of Personality* (1967), by courtesy of Charles C. Thomas, Publisher, Springfield, Ill.

In more recent psychological literature the emotional–non-emotional dimension has been relabelled in various ways: the stability dimension, the ego-strength dimension, etc.; and the changeable–unchangeable dimension is now usually referred to as the extraversion–introversion dimension, in deference to the terminology reintroduced and popularised by the psychologist C. G. Jung.[17] In line with the dual-dimensional schema illustrated in Figure 2, the former 'melancholic' temperament is reinterpreted as emotional-introverted, the 'sanguine' as non-emotional/extroverted, the 'choleric' as emotional-extroverted, and the 'phlegmatic' as non-emotional/introverted.

A great variety of tests have been devised by psychologists to measure these and other temperamental traits. In contemporary America, the great bulk of these tests have been developed for the psycho-physical evaluation of infants and young children by paediatricians, child psychiatrists and sociologists. In the assessment of adolescent and adult temperament, tests for extroversion and emotionality developed by Eysenck and others have been widely and successfully utilised. The National War College in Washington, DC, for example, uses the Myers-Briggs test for extroversion as a means for selecting the officers who will go on to the highest military positions (the preferred temperament is the Introvert-Sensing-Thinking-Judging type, which will presumably be least likely to start wars unnecessarily). St Louis University (Missouri) and other universities, routinely use the Myers-Briggs test to acquire a basic personality profile of their students. Some applications have also been made of the Sheldonian physique/temperament-typing system to medicine.[18]

Some of the research done with the extroversion–introversion and emotionality tests has a bearing on what we have called the 'aesthetic/moral' sphere of human experience. For instance, one can conclude from the research that extroverts are naturally more sociable[19] and also courageous (as a result of greater pain tolerance),[20] that introverts tend to avoid excesses with regard to sexual conduct[21] and the use of drugs,[22] and also to be more law-abiding,[23] and that those with 'stable' temperaments tend to conduct themselves well under conditions of acute stress.[24]

The Harvard physician-psychologist William H. Sheldon has taken a more independent direction in testing for the extrovert-introvert dimensions, dividing the extrovert 'type' into two sub-types, the affective extrovert and the active extrovert, and also hypothesising a positive correlation between temperament and physique. Because of his more subjective and not easily testable and replicable techniques for factoring out temperament traits, and possibly also because of a traditional reluctance on the part of American psychologists to admit any possibility that some aspects of human behaviour might be physically determined, and thus not subject to psychological intervention[25] – Sheldon's theory has elicited more controversy than any other contemporary temperament theory. However, some aspects of the theory have been corroborated,[26] and Sheldon's methods have been used with success in the study and 'typing' of children, adolescents, delinquents, and soldiers.[27] From the aesthetic/moral point of view, Sheldon's theory is interesting primarily as an interpretation of extroversion and introversion which develops in more concrete detail the differential orientations to behaviour that may be due to dispositions. For example, he supplements Eysenck's evidence about the resistance of introverts to drug abuse, with evidence that the extreme introvert ('cerebrotonic') has a natural aversion to drugs and alcohol;[28] he supplements other sources of information about extroversion with observations that the affective type of extroversion ('viscerotonic') has a kind of natural 'social intelligence', an unusual ability to tolerate differences of people and customs, and a particular interest in, and understanding of, young children;[29] and he finds that the active type of extroversion ('somatotonic') is associated not only with a kind of natural courage but also with an ability for making prudent, unsentimental decisions under stress.[30]

Is there anything corresponding to a male or female 'temperament'? Sheldon in his initial efforts to develop a methodology for typing individuals, had made just such an initial hypothesis, in addition to the hypotheses concerning the components of introversion and the components of the two types of extroversion. He expected that experimental evidence would corroborate the existence of a fourth component, 'gyandrophrenia', an independent cluster of M-F traits. But he was unable to find corroboration for this, and ended up with only the other three primary clusters of traits.[31] Numerous physiological and psychological studies of masculinity and femininity have been developed and used since Sheldon's early investigations, and some of these have indicated a possible linkup with aesthetic/moral values. For example, several studies have shown a 'correlation of plasma testosterone levels with aggressive behavior and social dominance in man'.[32] The evidence that females are characteristically less aggressive than males has been corroborated even by feminist psychologists,[33] who have been persistent and successful in discountenancing or questioning most assertions of feminine 'traits' which imply some sort of hereditary determination.[34] The evidence that females are indeed less aggressive, combined with similarly strong evidence of the greater verbal ability of females in general,[35] would seem to lead at least to the conservative conclusion that, if males because of aggressivity are naturally more disposed to the 'virtues' of self-assertiveness and accomplishment, females may be particularly oriented towards the resolution of disputes and conflicts through discussion, in a peaceful manner (a virtue of whose importance we are growing increasingly aware in the nuclear age).

Thus the question that is raised by the moral sense theories – 'just what are these "emotional orientations" that can be channelled naturally into ethical behaviour?' – is answered partially and tentatively by the concept of temperament. In terms of the S/O categories introduced at the beginning of this chapter, we could say that an individual's temperament will often give him or her a particularly strong impetus towards certain kinds of behaviour that also happen to be considered objectively fitting or correct, aside from considerations of temperament.

## 2(d) 2. Attempts to Ascertain Objective Aesthetic/Moral Standards

In the case of passive and active aesthetic experience, we saw that there were objective standards, set by society and/or by nature, to which the experience must correspond in order to be complete. For example, in a performing art such as ballet, the completeness of the experience of the passive spectator will depend to some extent on whether certain general standards are met, and the completeness of the experience of the dancers will depend on their following certain rules or techniques geared to producing the sort of performance that will be pleasing both to the artists themselves and to their audience. Many of the rules or standards in question here are conventional, that is, set by society, but for aesthetic experience in the wider sense, standards set by nature may also come into play. For example, if we include appreciation of the beauty of the opposite sex as an aesthetic experience, the norms here are set partly by societies (for example, in some societies heavy women are preferred to thin, certain types of ornamentation are worn that would be considered unattractive in Western European societies, etc.), partly by nature (there are presumably some racial or genetic factors that come into play in determining why we find some individuals more attractive than others).

Similarly we would expect that the aesthetic/moral orientations, manifested through a 'moral sense' or in a more specific way through some basic temperamental characteristics or personality traits, will be maximally fulfilling when they correspond to certain standards set by nature and/or society. If we possessed a moral sense, or a certain set of temperamental characteristics, what sort of objective norms for aesthetic/moral behaviour should be taken into account? The following three responses to this question are worth considering.

### 2(d) 2.1.   *Aesthetic/Moral Relativism*

'Relativism' in regard to behavioural norms is understood in a variety of ways: the descriptions given by anthropologists of the different moral norms in different cultures are called 'descriptive' relativism. Some philosophers have argued for 'normative' relativism,[36] that is, the view that the norms for each culture determine what is right and wrong. If we were to proceed further and argue that, because of conflicting norms in different cultures, there can be no such thing as 'right' and 'wrong', this would be 'meta-ethical' relativism.

Relativism in the normative and meta-ethical forms is particularly troublesome to ethicists insofar as it seems to introduce an unbridgeable gap between the 'is' and the 'ought', between the apparent extreme diversity of moral norms in different cultures, and the perennial endeavour of ethics to enunciate norms that are valid for all cultures.

*Aesthetic/moral* relativism, however, takes a more moderate and nuanced stance than normative and meta-ethical relativism. It merely states that the variety of norms we encounter in our socio-cultural environment supply us with a multiplicity of ways in which we can agreeably and creatively fulfil our natural attraction for behaving in socially approved ways. We are concerned here with the conventions of custom and etiquette, and also with some positive laws. Here there is really no 'ought' at all, at least not in the strong, categorical sense common to moral laws ('do not murder', etc.). The 'ought' here, being simply a socially acceptable expression of a natural disposition, is scarcely distinguishable from an 'is'. For example, I am gregarious by temperament; therefore, as frequently as I have the leisure, I seek out my friends (driving on the correct side of the street) for formal or informal get-togethers, in which I instinctively adhere to the written or unwritten rules of etiquette which have to do with avoiding unnecessary offence of others. Or I have a natural disposition for action and risk-taking; and so I get a job on the city Vice Squad, where I manage to avoid searches-without-warrant and bribe-taking, and still end up with moderate success in bringing underworld characters to justice.

What about situations in which certain types of behaviour which seem to us morally repugnant are universally approved within a certain culture? For example, the Spartans exposed newborns who were insufficiently robust on the mountainside; the Chulschi of Siberia killed the members of their tribe whom they considered to be too old; and some tribes in Africa routinely practised cannibalism. Even in comparatively modern times there have been practices of brutality or inhumanity (for example, slavery in the US and some Arabian countries, the persecution and abduction of Jews in Nazi Germany) which seem to have been accepted by the majority of the citizenry.

Behaviour corresponding to such 'repugnant' norms would, upon superficial examination, seem to qualify as aesthetic/moral. But it falls short of this for two reasons: (a) What psychological and anthropological knowledge we have does not seem to offer evidence that there could be a 'normal' attraction towards cannibalism, killing one's children, killing one's aged parents, or sadistically enslaving or eliminating outsiders. We may surmise that it is at least partially the emergence and triumph of normal human and humane dispositions that has gradually brought about a reversal of some of these perverse customs. (b) We have, of course, for purposes of analysis, been considering the aesthetic/moral sphere *in abstraction from the moral sphere*. And we may presume that most objective aesthetic/moral norms will not contravene objective moral norms (yet to be discussed). However, if and when the latter *are* contravened, the former are nullified, giving way to a more significant objectivity. This should become clearer as we examine the moral sphere, and its relation to the aesthetic/moral.

*2(d) 2.2.   Sociobiology; Reciprocal and Group Altruism*
As was indicated above, the objective norms in the aesthetic/moral
sphere may be established by society *and/or* by nature. The objective
norms which sociobiology is interested in seem to be of the sort
which are established *both* by society *and* by nature. We will begin
with an analysis, by a philosopher, of the norms established by
society, and then show how sociobiology tries to demonstrate how
the same or similar norms are indeed established by nature.

Henry Sidgwick in an important turn-of-the-century treatise gives
an analysis fo the development of a hierarchy of social norms
pertinent to what we have called here 'the aesthetic/moral sphere':

> We should all agree that each of us is bound to show kindness to
> his parents and spouse and children, and to other kinsmen in a
> less degree; and to those who have rendered services to him, and
> any others whom he may have admitted to his intimacy and called
> friends; and to neighbors and to fellow-countrymen more than to
> others; and perhaps we may say to those of our own race . . . ;
> and generally to human beings in proportion to their affinity to
> ourselves.[37]

During the 1970s a new science of 'sociobiology' emerged which,
as interpreted by its founder, Edward Wilson,[38] seems to indicate
that there is a natural, genetic basis for the general sort of
hierarchical ranking that Sidgwick refers to. Sociobiological
reasoning, which applies to all animals, including human beings, is
based on the laws of genetic transmission:

> Each child I produce contains half my genes; the other half of
> my children's genes comes, of course, from their mother. Each of
> my sisters and brothers will also, on average, have 50 per cent of
> the same genes as I have, since, like me, they have half of my
> mother's and half of my father's genes. (This 50 per cent is an
> average figure because, depending on how the genetic lottery fell
> out, they could have anything from all to none of their genes in
> common with me – but the huge number of genes involved makes
> either extreme unlikely.) . . . . The proportion of genes in
> common does fall off sharply as it becomes more distant –
> between aunts (or uncles) and their nieces (or nephews) it is 25 per
> cent; between first cousins 12½ per cent . . . .[39]

In other words, 'altruism' is a euphemism for 'selfish genes'! Following the laws of probability, sociobiology infers from these genetic facts a hierarchy in the degrees of altruism (for example, willingness to risk one's life to save another person). According to the genetic calculus of altruism, there would be an equal probability that an individual would be willing to risk his life for two children, two siblings, four nephews or nieces, or eight first cousins!

Sociobiology has been criticised for trying to work out formulas for human behaviour with mathematical exactitude,[40] but the fact that there is a genetic basis for *some* of the preferences and prejudices that Sidgwick recounts seems indisputable. Without drawing conclusions about the probabilities of the extremes of altruism, we might modestly conclude that humans have a genetic orientation (which can be modified or obstructed in complex ways through other orientations), which disposes them to give greater weight to the needs, interests, desires, perhaps also values, of those to whom they are closely related 'by blood'.

To explain the *non*-kinship relationships mentioned at the outset of this section by Sidgwick, we would have to supplement the genetic considerations of sociobiology with the general zoological principle of 'reciprocal altruism' – you do a favour for me (for example, scratch my back), and I reciprocate – and with the extrapolated principle of 'group altruism' – we do give special consideration to members of our group (or race, or nation), and use exclusionary tactics on outsiders, who might take advantage of our own system of mutual benefits.[41]

These principles – still somewhat speculative and tentative – at least adumbrate the possibility that some of the objective norms for aesthetic/moral behaviour may be grounded in biology and ethology, as well as anthropology.

We turn now to developmental psychology to consider a final possibility that there are some objective norms which may be attributable to psychological causes.

### 2(d) 2.3.  *Kohlberg's Theory of Moral Development*

When we speak about objective norms for aesthetic/moral behaviour, we have to include, at least implicitly, expectations concerning what is 'normal' for particular stages in human development. Kohlberg's theory,[42] which offers evidence that there are, indeed, definable stages in moral development from late childhood to adulthood, raises the possibility that the differential behavioural expectations directed towards children and adults, respectively, may be derived not only from society but also from nature.

Kohlberg's theory, based on a longitudinal study of development from late childhood through adulthood, differentiates three levels and six stages of moral development, according to the following schema:[43]

| Level | Stage |
|---|---|
| Pre-conventional morality | 1. Obedience under threat of punishment<br>2. Intermittent egoism and pragmatic altruism |
| Conventional morality | 3. Conformity; desire to please<br>4. Orientation to maintain authority and social order |
| Post-conventional morality | 5. Consciousness of commitments to a 'social contract'<br>6. Emphasis on conscience and moral principles |

Carol Gilligan, a Harvard colleague and former collaborator with Kohlberg, has alleged that these Kohlbergian stages are more representative for male moral development than for female. She offers evidence that female development emphasises a more *contextual*, relational approach, less of the formal, principled orientation than is exemplified especially by Kohlberg's final two 'stages'.[44] The ongoing debate about whether there really is some gender-bias built into the Kohlbergian hierarchy seems to hinge largely on diverse interpretations of the data, possibly conditioned by allegiances to diverse theories of morality.[45] However, it is conceivable that some modification of the above-mentioned sequential stages may eventually result from further research in developmental psychology.

In the meantime, numerous cross-cultural studies have confirmed Kohlberg's findings concerning the first two levels (stages 1–4).[46] At least with regard to these two levels, we are presented with objective aesthetic/moral norms which seem to be not only based on universal social expectations but rooted in nature, that is, the natural sequential development of human consciousness. Thus, for example, if a young adult behaves habitually in accord with a punishment-orientation, we consider this abnormal; but if a ten-year-old behaves similarly, we (that is, society, including scientific interpreters of nature, like Kohlberg) consider this tolerable, if not optimal. In the latter case, neither the active aesthetic/moral experience of the ten-year-old, nor the passive aesthetic/moral experience of those who deal with him or her, need be disturbed in any substantial way.

It is interesting to note that the last two '*post*-conventional' stages were attained by only a minority of Kohlberg's subjects, and that cross-cultural studies have shown these stages to be scarcely ever attained in other cultures. For the post-conventional level – the last stage especially – represents a transition from the objective norms of the aesthetic/moral to those of the moral sphere, from conventional expectations to a more critical stance. Thus we are led paradoxically by Kohlberg's study of *normal* development to an infrequently attained but not insignificant level of psychological development concerned with going *beyond* mere 'normality' and with being *post*-conventional. It is to be hoped that we may find the denizens of this level to be more numerous than appeared to be the case with Kohlberg's subjects.

# 3
# Moral Good

## ARGUMENT

*Behaviour or decision-making on the specifically moral plane, although it may not constitute the major portion of everyday life for 'everyman', is of major philosophical interest, if only because it promises to give us some deeper insights into human nature, and possibly into some new guidelines for the greater fulfilment and/or perfection of the individual and society. Many theories concerned with the interpretation of specifically moral behaviour fall, in terms of relative emphasis, into one of the following two groupings: (1) theories concerned with the determination of the proper subjective dispositions for moral decision-making or moral behaviour; and (2) theories concerned with the disclosure or discovery of certain objective norms applicable to human behaviour. The first type of theory is based on an implicit or explicit theory of philosophical anthropology, which has to do with the question concerning the specific distinction of human beings from the other animals – e.g. are human beings distinguished specifically by rationality? and how is 'rationality' defined? The answers given will have an effect on the subjectively oriented moral theory connected with that position (or a combination including that position) in philosophical anthropology. The second type of theory is based on certain scientific, metaphysical or sociopolitical presuppositions which carry with them implications or corollaries in regard to the way people in general should act.*

*This meta-theoretical analysis will provide a framework for a final brief consideration of the possibility and desirability of a 'correlative' ethical theory, and also show how moral theorising begins to converge with religious and theological views concerning human behaviour.*

---

Those of us who use the English language may be somewhat hampered and unconsciously prejudiced by a long-standing

English tradition concerning the connotation of 'moral'. Mary Midgley has shown that the common English usage of 'moral', largely because of the influence of Dr Samuel Johnson (1709–84), has come to emphasise external, habitual, conventional behaviour.[1] This usage contrasts remarkably with that of the most influential continental moral philosopher, Kant, who emphasises subjective intentions and 'good will' as the essence of morality. Thus, for example, while the English philosopher J. S. Mill in his *Essay on Liberty*, ch. iv, contrasts the *private* sphere of the liberty of individual conscience with the sphere of 'morality or law', Kant tells us in his *Groundwork for a Metaphysic of Morals*, ch. i, that only with a good intention 'would [a person's] conduct first acquire moral worth'. In the twentieth century, G. E. Moore, whose questions concerning the nature of the good set off a train of investigations which are still continuing, was undaunted by Kant's attempt to emphasise the subjectivity of morality, and habitually favoured the Johnsonian usage, applying the word 'moral' generally to external imperatives followed largely without thought.[2]

The identification of the moral with the *public* and *social* is perhaps most evident now in contemporary Anglo-American utilitarianism, in which 'utility' has become almost synonymous with 'social utility', and morality is taken to be teleologically ordered to furthering such utility. This usage, however, is not confined to the utilitarians, but is also prevalent even among utilitarianism's critics. Thus, for example, David Gauthier, in a recent rebuttal of utilitarianism, nevertheless accepts utilitarian terminology regarding 'a positive and impartial link between personal and moral [sic] preference'.[3]

Some writers have proceeded from this sort of usage to an explicit ideological justification of the essentially social nature of morality. Thus John Dewey asserts, 'If a man lived alone in the world there might be some sense in the question "Why be moral?" were it not for one thing: No such question would then arise.' For in Dewey's estimation morality is unthinkable aside from a social context.[4] Kurt Baier renews the Deweyan challenge, arguing that there is simply no morality for a Robinson Crusoe, since such a person would have no *social* obligations.[5] In a recent book, Stuart Hampshire, who allows for a sphere of private morality, nevertheless, possibly unintentionally, subordinates this sphere to the public sphere when he argues that only public officials have to give *reasons* for moral choices.[6] (One wonders whether the continuing strength of intuitionist theories, including Hampshire's, in contemporary ethics might not be due to some such unconscious subordination of a capricious private sphere to the public, where morality in the *strict* sense, a *serious* matter for which *reasons* must be given, reigns.)

This interpretation of 'moral' as social and public has some etymological justification, in so far as 'moral' is derived from the Latin, *mos* ('custom'), just as 'ethical' is derived from the Greek, *ethos* ('custom'). But Greek and Roman ethicists, as I will show, rose above this conventional usage; and many modern philosophers have gone even beyond the ancient Greek and Roman philosophers in emphasising the importance of individual subjectivity and the existence of duties to oneself, as well as others.

In opposition to the trend of interpreting morality as exclusively social, Henry Veatch argues that, if we took Baier's assertion literally, we should be forced into the absurd conclusion that morality has nothing to do with furthering our own ends and purposes, and we should have to reject completely Socrates' claim that morality is primarily a matter of self-knowledge.[7] This would be to abandon the basic insights and principles which gave rise to the development of ethical theory in Western philosophy in the first place.

Dewey, in his concentration on the social aspects of morality, is willing to grant at least some importance to motives, conceived not as some inner nucleus of freedom, but as a disposition or tendency to act (in a socially beneficial manner).[8] Social utilitarians, however, are most uncompromising in their downgrading of the subjective element, focusing so intensively on the social consequences of behaviour that inner intentions or motives are for all practical purposes irrelevant. In this orientation they are comparable to the behaviourist school of psychology, which would like to isolate various 'objective' aspects of behaviour, and have nothing whatever to do with motives or intentions, which are considered vague, quasi-mystical, and, in any case, unobservable.

But any attempt to confine oneself just to the measurable aspects or the ascertainable consequences of behaviour must end up losing sight of human behaviour itself. As Alasdair MacIntyre points out, 'There is no such thing as "behavior," to be identified prior to and independently of intentions, beliefs, and settings.'[9] Indeed, it is hard to conceive of behaviour which could be properly interpreted and assessed, without any knowledge of intentions or motives. MacIntyre gives the example of a stranger who walks up to you at the bus stop and tells you 'The name of the common wild duck is *Histrionicus histrionicus histrionicus*'. This is behaviour that could be variously interpreted as a case of mistaken identity, or as some new psychiatric therapy for shyness, or as the passing on of a code word by a spy, etc., etc.[10] You would have to know something about intentions in order to categorise it at all. In more specifically ethical behaviour, the same sort of problem obtains. If a young man helps an old lady across the street, this might be an act of gallantry; or a manoeuvre by a robber to get the lady out of the way of the entrance to a bank, so that there will be no obstruction when the getaway car pulls up for some of his accomplices; or as a move to get the old lady out of earshot so that he can solicit prostitutes on the corner without being discovered; etc.

It is of course possible to go to the opposite extreme, emphasising subjective intentions to such an extent that, it would seem, these intentions could 'baptise' some rather questionable ethical decisions (some examples will be given in section (a) 2.5 below). I have concentrated on the objective extreme, since long-standing traditions and linguistic usage make this latter extreme more attractive and easier to lapse into, at least in the Anglo-American cultural context. (The above critique of objectivism does not encompass 'meta-ethical objectivism', which is an extreme objectivist interpretation of linguistic usage, and which is beyond the scope of the present study.)

Our analysis of aesthetic and aesthetic/moral experience in the preceding chapter emphasised a correlative subjective/objective approach as the best means for highlighting the essentials of the experience in question, without lapsing into a tenuous and self-defeating extreme subjectivism or objectivism. We will proceed in the present chapter to examine some predominantly subjective and predominantly objective approaches to morality, and then some attempts at correlativism. But first it will be necessary to compare moral with aesthetic/moral experience, in order to differentiate the two spheres most effectively, and to show in just what respects the moral goes beyond the aesthetic/moral.

The aesthetic/moral sphere, as we saw, is concerned with channelling natural dispositions, propensities, abilities or talents into behaviour which will correspond to objective norms, derived either from nature or society. As we examine instances of behaviour which result in 'incomplete' aesthetic/moral good, however, we begin to realise a necessity for going beyond the aesthetic/moral sphere. For example, I may do something objectively desirable which goes counter to my dispositions; or I may do something which appeals to non-conventional standards of objectivity. In either case, the aesthetic/moral good is lacking, *but* the action may still be good in the strictly *moral* sense.

Although aesthetic/moral experience bears no constitutional deficiencies in itself, it is subject to two major deficiencies from the point of view of total human experience.

*Subjectively speaking*, the dependence of aesthetic/moral behaviour on certain congruent inclinations or propensities to a great extent *limits* the scope of human behaviour, ruling out a great range of admirable acts that are said to be made possible through human freedom or some characteristic excellence of human nature. Thus – to borrow a couple of examples from Kant[11] – a tradesman's natural feelings of benevolence towards his customers may keep him honest in transactions, but what if his customers are gullible or obnoxious? And a man's natural inclination to preserve his life will be enough to keep him from suicide, but what if adversity and hopeless sorrow have completely taken away his relish for life? – In such situations of temptation, stress or adversity, which enter into the lives of most human beings, something stronger than aesthetic/moral dispositions will be required to make further moral progress possible.

Likewise, the *objective* norms for aesthetic/moral behaviour, often set and reinforced by the community, can be equally restrictive, from a broader moral point of view. John Dewey describes some of these 'objective' limitations clearly and concretely in his analysis of 'conventional morality':

> 'Conventional morality' is precisely a morality of praise and blame based on the code of valuations which happens to be current at a particular time in a particular social group. Whatever conforms, at least outwardly, to current practices, especially those of an institutional sort, receives commendation or at least passes without censure; whatever deviates exposes one to censure. . . .
>
> Thus a militant community admires and extols all warlike achievements and traits; an industrialized community sets store by thrift, calculations, constancy of labor, and applauds those persons who exhibit these qualities. . . .[12]

Dewey concludes that we must go beyond such norms (which we have called 'aesthetic/moral') through 'reflection', a more critical relationship to our social environment.

If there are also objective aesthetic/moral norms established by *nature*, these may also be restrictive, even stifling. Even if, for example, the sociobiologists are correct regarding our propensity to give preference to those who are most similar to us in gene make-up, surely we must go beyond such propensities to assure anything like human moral progress.

But *why* go beyond such objective narrowness and the narrow ranges of human inclinations and dispositions that impel us to action? More fundamentally, *can* we go beyond such things? *Do* we, in actual practice?

With such questions we come to the larger question of the nature of moral good. For it is presumably for the sake of moral good that we are willing to go beyond the scope of aesthetic/moral aspirations and objectives. But to tell us that the moral goes beyond the aesthetic is not to say much about it. What are the positive characteristics of the moral good? In particular, in those instances where the pursuit of morality means leaving the aesthetic sphere almost completely behind, how can morality still be 'good' in any meaningful way?

In order to answer these questions, I shall begin with a brief sketch of the subjective and objective aspects of moral good, and some initial examples of the subjective/objective dynamics. Then, having provided at least a general introduction to the subjective/objective dynamics of moral good, I shall go on to an analysis of moral theories exemplifying some more sophisticated elaborations of both the subjective and objective aspects.

*Subjective prerequisites for the moral good:* Here I am no longer talking about the simple attractions, inclinations, or dispositions whose limitations Kant was concerned with. I am concerned with what are widely agreed to be higher human qualities – rationality, freedom, self-consciousness, and/or an orientation towards society. These qualities, self-consciousness particularly, but possibly also some of the others, may be peculiar to man, as I have argued elsewhere.[13] But whether or not we share some or all of these qualities with other animals, most of us in our better moments would consider some of them to be 'higher' – that is, more significant, more intimately connected with what it means to be human. For those who concur with this insight, the preservation, elaboration and furtherance of these qualities is, indeed, essential to happiness, is even attractive in a fundamental sense (*pace* Kant), and is the subjective prerequisite for the attainment of the moral good.

*Objective aspects of the moral good:* Granted that, as Dewey suggested, any 'reflective' person must go beyond the conventional norms set by the community or even the nation, and granted that we must sometimes go beyond some 'natural' biological, psychological, or sociological norms (for example, sociobiological laws, if such laws exist) – what is to take their place? Presumably, some objective norms more fundamental than the former, and thus able to supersede them. Thus, in place of the conventional norms of 'tribal morality', our attention is sometimes directed by ethical theorists to standards elaborated by society in a larger sense, even mankind in general. Some theorists even see the continual enlargement of the range of our moral attitudes beyond the tribal and the provincial as an incessant process connected with social evolution.[14] And if there are also some objective norms dictated by *nature*, the long-standing 'natural law' tradition in ethics is concerned with ferreting out the most fundamental norms – norms which may or may not be reinforced by society. If there do exist such general and all-embracing norms, presumably it is important that human beings not contradict them in any radical way, and presumably human fulfilment ('happiness' in the objective sense) will be enhanced by conformity to them. Thus they would also constitute the objective prerequisites for complete moral good.

The importance of both the subjective and the objective aspects for the attainment of moral good is illustrated in the following chart. This chart, like those used to illustrate subjective/objective dynamics in the aesthetic and aesthetic/moral spheres, concentrates on extreme examples to highlight the polarities involved. It is presumed that most moral activity will be comfortably situated at some distance from such extremes:

| Subjective disposition (moral intention) | Objective conformity (universal moral standards) | Result |
|---|---|---|
| A businessman is interested only in profits, but is afraid of losing his reputation for honesty | He joins the Better Business Bureau and the Rotary Club and follows their rules inculcating honest business practices | Incomplete moral good (deficient SD) |
| A university student is interested only in his own freedom and pursuing his own rights, but also wants to belong to some group in which there are many attractive members of the opposite sex | The student joins a human-rights group and travels with them to a foreign country to investigate human rights violations | Incomplete MG (deficient SD) |
| As President of the United States, I initiate a nuclear war to prevent the inhibition of individual liberty by atheistic communism | All living things except cockroaches are destroyed by a 'nuclear winter', and the human impulse to self-preservation is frustrated | Incomplete MG (deficient OC) |
| As a politician from one of the best and most highly educated families, I do everything I can to make sure that wealth and power in my country remains in the hands of 'good-quality' people | The great majority of people in my country, who are impoverished, unrefined and uneducated, suffer immensely as a result of my policies and enactments | Incomplete MG (deficient OC) |
| Martha follows the 'Golden Rule' in her private and public dealings | In the international sphere, she works for the more equitable distribution of the world's resources between the highly industrialised countries and the 'third world' | Moral good |

## 3(a) ATTEMPTS TO ASCERTAIN AND/OR PROMOTE SUBJECTIVE DISPOSITIONS CONGRUENT TO MORALITY

As was indicated above, the determination of the dispositions pertinent to morality is related to a great extent to an interpretation of human nature. Once one decides what there is that is specifically 'human', some conclusions concerning human behaviour will ordinarily follow. Even if one admits no 'difference in kind' between man and the other animals (that is, no important human quality completely lacking in animals), but only a 'difference in degree' – for example, greater sociability – some conclusions might be entailed. But the sharpest conclusions concerning moral behaviour are entailed by certain positions which maintain a difference-in-kind between human and non-human animals.

Among those who argue for a species-specific human difference-in-kind, divergent interpretations have arisen. Some maintain that the key human characteristic is rationality, others that it is freedom, or some other attribute. After a moral philosopher has singled out, or assented to, some essential differentiating human characteristic, he will very often devise some means or method for ascertaining the existence of that characteristic.

In the following analysis, we will consider some procedures or 'tests' that have arisen in moral philosophy in connection with some of the chief views concerning the difference-in-kind between man and the other animals:

### 3(a) 1.   Procedures for Ascertaining/Promoting Self-Determination

Self-determination is often equated with human free will. It is perhaps best understood from what it denies. It denies that human beings are completely determined by their material make-up, their inclinations or passions, or their environment. It holds that humans can and do in some way rise above such things, and are causes of their own behaviour: self-determiners, self-conditioners. Some have described this condition as 'autonomy' (being determined by oneself), in contrast to 'heteronomy' (being determined by something other than oneself). But for the authors we will consider, it would almost be misleading to state that one 'ought' to rise to autonomy, as if one could be a bona fide human being, and still have no autonomy. For to lack autonomy is taken by them to be for all practical purposes a renunciation of humanity, *de jure*, or at least *de facto*.

### 3(a) 1.1.   *Plato: Gyges' Ring*

**[The shepherd, Gyges, found a magic gold ring and wore it to an assembly of shepherds.] He chanced to turn the collet of the ring**

inside his hand, when instantly he became invisible to the rest of the company. . . . Suppose now that there were two such magic rings, and a just man put on one of them and an unjust man the other; no man can be imagined to be of such an iron nature that he would stand fast in justice. No man would keep his hands off what was not his own when he could safely take what he liked out of the market, or go into houses and lie with any one at his pleasure, or kill or release from prison whom he would, and in all respects be like a God among men. Then the actions of the just would be as the actions of the unjust; they would both come at last to the same point.[15]

In this excerpt from a dialogue between Socrates and Glaucon in the *Republic*, Glaucon presents Socrates with a fascinating challenge: if we were ever truly invisible (like Gyges in the legend), and there were no danger of our ever being detected, could we avoid the temptation to take sexual liberties, or liberties with the property of others?

To go beyond the examples offered by Glaucon – could we ignore the opportunity to get access to secret information that would give us an advantage in our business life, or our personal or social life, or simply satisfy our curiosity? And if we would not stoop to injuring or killing our enemies, what about putting a few well-placed obstacles in their way? And so forth.

The challenge to morality or 'justice' is clear: what seems to be upright, moral behaviour may be simply the result of fear – fear of being detected, fear of losing one's reputation, fear of being punished. If this is the case, there is no particular merit in being moral. If one person seems to be more moral than another, this may be because he is more fearful, or have more to fear.

In Plato's dialogue, Socrates answers Glaucon's challenge by saying that even if one had Gyges' ring, it would be in his self-interest to do what is right, to do the good. And what sort of good would bolster one against all the temptations induced by being invisible and unassailable? Later on in the dialogue,[16] Socrates gets more specific about the good he has in mind: it is the internal harmony of a soul which is not beset by unruly passions and desires, but has them firmly in control, and truly is able to determine itself on the basis of rational choices. By giving in to desires which are unworthy of a rational being, even an invisible possessor of Gyges' ring would lose his self-respect, and, what is even more important, lose his power of self-determination – his freedom – even if no one were ever to apprehend him.

For someone who would be quite contented with an abundance of non-moral, 'aesthetic' goods, it would be hard to accept Socrates' reasoning. But for someone who is living and thinking on the moral level, the reasoning is almost self-evident: the possession of something like Gyges' ring would not be an insuperable challenge, but a once-in-a-lifetime *opportunity* to gain some relatively unassailable proof of a species of good conceivable and attainable by human beings alone – the power of self-determination.

### 3(a) 1.2. Kant: the Notion of Duty

The notion of duty . . . includes that of a good will, although implying certain subjective restrictions. These [restrictions], however, far from concealing [good will] or rendering it unrecognizable, rather bring it out by contrast and make it shine forth so much the brighter.

[a] I omit here all actions which are already recognized as inconsistent with duty. . . . [b] I also set aside those actions which really conform to duty, but to which men have *no* direct *inclination*, performing them because they are impelled thereto by some other inclination. . . . [c] It is much harder to make [a distinction between action done from duty, and action done from other motives] when the action accords with duty, and the subject has besides a *direct* inclination to it. For example . . . it is a duty to maintain one's life; and in addition, everyone has also a direct inclination to do so. But on this account the often anxious care which most men take for it has no intrinsic worth, and their maxim [to preserve their life] has no moral import. . . . On the other hand, [d] if adversity and hopeless sorrow have completely taken away the relish for life, if the unfortunate one . . . yet preserves his life . . . from duty – then his maxim has moral worth.[17]

In the above passage, (part [c]) Kant argues that if we have a direct inclination to do something which also happens to be our duty, it has little or no moral worth. Actually he seems to waver between 'little' and 'no'. He begins by saying it is much '*harder*' to make the distinction between moral and amoral behaviour in such cases, but in the example given – preservation of one's life when one is inclined thereto – he states categorically that the action 'has *no* moral worth'.

In addition to the example included in the above excerpt, he gives elsewhere the example of a tradesman who deals honestly with his customers because 'his own advantage requires it',[18] and concludes that the tradesman's honesty 'is not enough to make us believe that the tradesman has so acted from duty . . .'.[19] Here Kant merely manifests some incredulity, but in still another example he is more emphatic: The example is that of a philanthropist who is generous and likes being generous, concerning whom Kant concludes that the generosity has 'no true moral worth'.

Before going any further, let us take note of a two-tiered ambiguity in Kant's analysis: (1) Kant himself calls our attention to a first-order ambiguity concerning the moral value of performing duties which are also pleasant (the type of activity we designated 'aesthetic/moral' in the preceding chapter); (2) and *we* also notice in *Kant* a certain second-order ambiguity as to whether such actions are just lacking in 'credibility', and 'harder' to designate as moral, *or* definitely 'have no moral worth'. Let us focus separately on each of these two types of ambiguity.

(1) In accord with our concept of aesthetic/moral behaviour introduced earlier, we would have to conclude that such behaviour is *essentially* ambiguous from the moral point of view. For this is precisely the sphere where there is a continual interplay between aesthetic and more strictly moral interests and activities. But Kant, as a moralist trying to isolate the essential characteristics of morality, is not content with indicating an ambiguity. Besides, an ambiguity between possibility $x$ and possibility $y$ cannot be fully understood unless we have a clear idea of each possibility. And 'possibility $y$' in this case is morality. We need to form a clear idea of what it means to be moral, by in some sense isolating morality for a better view.

(2) Kant, however, has some natural hesitation about stating categorically, 'doing your duty has moral worth only if you don't enjoy it'. This is the sort of position that has given moralists – before and after Kant – a bad reputation, and led to the pejorative use of the term 'moralistic'. On the other hand, he *is* interested in introducing a clear and distinct idea of the nature of moral behaviour; and how can this be done with regard to aesthetic/moral behaviour, where there is an essential ambiguity of moral/amoral motivation? The ambiguity must at least be pointed out. And so he introduces a few contingent examples of aesthetic/moral behaviour which 'have no moral value', but does not go quite so far as to formulate the general principle, 'an action can have moral value only if we don't enjoy it'.

A way out of Kant's apparent difficulty may be found, if we can be allowed to call attention to, and resolve, a *third-order* ambiguity, between the metaphysical and epistemological levels. The statement, 'behaviour that we enjoy cannot be moral' is a metaphysical statement, and is deservedly subject to criticism for excessive moralism. But the statement, 'behaviour that we enjoy cannot be *called* moral with any absolute *certitude*' is epistemological in its bearings. It merely takes note of the aforesaid ambiguity of aesthetic/moral behaviour, and indicates that if one wanted to have a clear and distinct concept of pure morality, he would simply have to do away with the ambiguity by focusing on the clear-cut cases, in which the sense of duty goes very much against the inclinations.

The resolution of the ambiguity between the metaphysical and the epistemological levels in Kant is then possible if we are willing to interpret his apparently metaphysical statements in an epistemological way, so that '*x* has no moral worth' is taken to mean '*x* cannot be certified to have moral worth'. This latter reading seems to be congruent with Kant's intentions, since he clearly avoids generalising that 'no enjoyable duties can have moral worth'.

Taken in this epistemological sense, Kant's statements about duty and inclination may be taken as a sophisticated test for self-determination. Arguing in the spirit of Kant, we may pose the question: if one were to spend one hundred per cent of his time on the aesthetic/moral level, never having to struggle with himself, never needing to go against his inclinations for the sake of duty, how could he be *sure* that he was, in fact, determining himself, and was not simply borne along by the ebb and flow of 'natural' inclinations? If he is in fact capable of true self-determination, true freedom, this can best be ascertained in those instances where he is able to go against or rise above his inclinations; and there is even a certain direct proportionality involved, in so far as the degree of certitude of self-determination is proportional to the degree of adversity that is overcome.

This idea, of course, leaves itself open to a number of criticisms: when we seem to be 'going against our inclinations', perhaps we are just masochists (who seem to have an *inclination* to 'go against their inclinations') or perhaps we are influenced unconsciously by social pressures to do so (and thus are not really 'determining' ourselves). But to criticise in this fashion would be to expect too much probative force from what amounts to a simple psychological experiment.

The Kantian experiment, however, goes beyond the sort of thought-experiment adumbrated by Plato's Gyges' ring device. A *mere* thought-experiment – would I be able to perform such-and-such duties under conditions of great adversity? – would presumably not be enough, if one is to pass the Kantian test. An individual would have to be actually faced with the conflicts and contradictions, in order to gain a satisfactory degree of certitude concerning his power of self-determination of which he has some intimations. And to a moral individual, such certitude about being in control of his life would be a form of happiness, although some might substitute another term (as, for example, Kant substitutes 'the pure feeling of respect for duty'[20]). If we were to insist categorically that *no* happiness could be involved in such moral experience, we find ourselves championing the sort of caricature of morality that Schiller pokes fun at, with Kantianism in mind:

> [Disciple:] Willingly serve I my friends, but I do it, alas, with affection. Hence I am plagued with this doubt, virtue I have not attained.
>
> [Master:] This is your only resource, you must stubbornly seek to abhor them; Then you can do with disgust that which the law may enjoin.[21]

### 3(a) 1.3. *Sartre: Good Faith*

**Ontology and existential psychoanalysis (or the spontaneous and empirical application which men have always made of these disciplines) must reveal to the moral agent that he is *the being by whom values exist*. It is then that his freedom will become conscious of itself and will reveal itself in anguish as the unique source of value and the nothingness by which the world exists.**

**Freedom, in respect of concrete circumstances, can have no other end and aim but itself. . . . Freedom [is] the foundation of all values. . . . The actions of men of good faith have, as their ultimate significance, the quest of freedom itself as such.[22]**

The existentialist philosopher Jean-Paul Sartre (1905–80) begins with the ordinary meaning of 'good faith' and 'bad faith' in common parlance, and then proceeds to his existential analysis. The ordinary meaning of 'bad faith' is 'insincerity' or duplicity, and as applied to an individual's relation to himself (for example, in religious hypocrisy) it means 'self-deception'. 'Good faith', on the other hand, connotes 'sincerity' with oneself and others. Sartre goes on from these meanings to pose the question: whether a person could really deceive himself. In a way, the concept of self-deception is an astonishing idea, because it seems to imply that I could consciously propose a lie to myself and then unconsciously be duped by my own fabrications. Freud avoided such an inconvenient impasse by relying completely on the hypothesis of an 'unconscious', which exerts a kind of causal influence on the psyche, without our knowing for certain that we are the sources of the unconscious content. But such explanations, for Sartre, smack of escapism and irresponsibility. Even if we had an unconscious, we must become conscious of it, and take responsibility for it. Why? Because nothing is more important than our freedom, and our freedom gives us the power of transcending all such determinisms.

Instead of resorting to an 'unconscious' then, Sartre explains 'bad faith' in terms of quite conscious subterfuges geared towards distracting us from our freedom. The following three subterfuges are especially prevalent and noteworthy:

3(a) 1.31.  *Taking refuge in a 'role'*: Sartre gives the example of a waiter who throws himself into his role completely, identifies with all the mannerisms, the hustle-bustle, the punctiliousness and the discretion that a good waiter is 'supposed' to have – to such an extent that his private personality seems to be defined by the same parameters.[23] There is little or no need for freedom, because all free decisions are dictated by his role. And in general a person can use any role recognised by society, or some subgroup of society – housewife, politician, policeman, soldier – as an escape from the exercise of personal freedom. The moral dangers of this escape become particularly clear, when the role becomes an obstacle to free decision – for example, when a soldier who is commanded to carry out an inhumane act can only avoid the inhumaneness by acting 'unsoldierly', or when one has become so identified with a role that he or she is at a loss outside of it – for example, when a veteran politician finally loses an election and simply cannot bear the idea of becoming just a 'private citizen'.

3(a) 1.32.  *Ignoring threats to one's freedom*: Sartre gives the example of a woman who dates a man for the first time and gradually is confronted with words, actions, and touches which are clearly oriented to seduction.[24] But she chooses to ignore the intention which is becoming apparent; she focuses only on the acts themselves, and chooses to interpret them as signs of high regard for her 'person'. She does not want to believe that she might be taken just as an object for sexual conquest by the man, and so she makes herself 'unconscious', for all practical purposes, about what is really going on. And thus, in general, our ability freely to ignore threats to our freedom, that is, compromising situations, is itself a great overarching threat to freedom.

3(a) 1.33. *Failure to take responsibility for one's acts:* In times past, religion offered to many a subterfuge, through which they could avoid personal responsibility. In our day, one of the most secure ways of avoiding personal responsibility is through recourse to scientific explanations of one's behaviour. Sartre gives the example of a woman who, because of loss of interest in her spouse, consciously does things during sexual intercourse that will distract her from enjoyment, and is exonerated from her responsibility for this by a psychoanalyst's diagnosis of sexual 'frigidity'.[25] Another more metaphysical way of avoiding responsibility would be through 'transcendence' of the past – for example, a man's refusal to take responsibility for certain offences committed in the past, on the grounds that he is now a changed person, and shouldn't have to be affected by past mistakes.[26] And so an act, whether past or present or future, can easily be disowned (along with our freedom), if we resort to the numerous explanations and justifications (including many respectable and even scientifically acceptable explanations and justifications) available to us.

'Good faith', or 'authenticity' (a term which Sartre came to use as a synonym), in contrast, means acting for freedom, with full consciousness of positive and negative possibilities for expressing our freedom, and with a generous insistence on taking responsibility for our acts even when society is willing to excuse us for them. But even if we act in 'good faith', according to the Sartrean definition, we should not expect to avoid all ambiguity and be presented with clear-cut choices. An example given by Sartre in *Existentialism is a Humanism* helps to illustrate this: A young man is faced with the choice of either going off to join the resistance movement for the liberation of his country, or staying home to care for his sick mother. There is no predetermined or automatic decision-procedure for such cases. The young man may decide that he has a primary responsibility to his mother, or he may decide that joining the resistance will best guarantee the freedom of all, including his mother. Whatever he chooses, the only important thing is that he choose freely, with as much knowledge as possible of relevant circumstances, and take full responsibility for the choice once made.

Sartre himself gives us some good examples of the practical implications of his theories in some of his own personal choices: refusing to marry and accept the role of 'husband'; refusing the Nobel Prize for Literature in 1964 (a threat to his uncompromising independence); a free and responsible relationship to his lifelong companion, Simone de Beauvoir, in spite of (Sartre might say 'because of') the absence of any institutional matrimonial ties, etc. Even his complex and controversial support of Marxism, which has been thought by many to go counter to his individualist, 'existentialist' principles, seems, at least in view of the arguments of Sartre's *Critique of Dialectical Reason* (1976), to be an application of the principle of the furtherance of freedom (in this case, freedom from the determinisms of scarcity and hunger throughout the world).

### 3(a) 2. Procedures for Ascertaining/Promoting Rationality

'Rationality' has multiple meanings in ordinary language and also in philosophy. Sometimes it means universalisation (the power to go beyond particular instances to form universal rules); sometimes logical self-consistency (non-self-contradiction); sometimes the ability to distinguish means from ends and to utilise suitable means to attain one's ends. It can also mean objectivity – the impartial, unbiased examination of the facts relevant to a situation; moderation, in the sense of the avoidance of unseemly excesses of emotion or passion; and/or sublimation, the ability to channel impulses and passions in humanly feasible ways. Each of the following moral theories is concerned with explicating one or more of these facets or aspects of rationality.

*3(a) 2.1. The Golden Rule: Universality, Self-Consistency and Means–End Subordination*

**What is hateful to you, do not do to your neighbour. (Judaism)**

**As you would that men should do to you, do ye also to them likewise. (Christianity)**

**What you do not want done to yourself, do not do unto others.    (Confucianism)**

**Let no man do to another that which would be repugnant to himself.    (Hinduism)**

**Hurt not others in ways that you yourself would find hurtful.    (Buddhism)**[27]

The various versions of the 'Golden Rule' cited above are notable above all for their emphasis on self-consistency. Self-consistency in its pure logical form is a combination of the principle of non-self-contradiction (you cannot simultaneously both affirm that an object $x$ has the property $F$ [the affirmation is symbolised as $F(x)$], and deny that $x$ has $F$ [the denial is symbolised $NF(x)$]), with the principle of identity ($F(x)$ implies $F(x)$ implies $F(x)$ *ad infinitum* ['a rose is a rose is a rose . . .']). The various negative versions of the Golden Rule (Judaism, Confucianism, Buddhism, Hinduism) emphasise non-self-contradiction: it is unthinkable, a travesty of logic, to do something to someone that you would not want done to yourself. The positive (Christian) form emphasises the principle of identity; if you have a right which you think someone should recognise, it is only logical for you to recognise that same right in the other person. It is doubtful whether 'desire' could be substituted for 'right'; this would be to go beyond the realm of mutual duties to supererogatory acts, which are really not subject to rules. And as long as we read the Christian form as applying only to 'rights', not 'desires' – the positive and negative forms are equivalent to each other, in the same way that in formal logic the law of identity entails the law of non-self-contradiction ($[F(x) \rightarrow F(x)] \rightarrow N[F(x)$ and $NF(x)]$). (Note: 'implies' is symbolised as '$\rightarrow$'. Quantifiers are omitted in these simple applications of formal logic.)

The question may arise: what if someone imagines s/he has a right which s/he really doesn't have, for example, the right to some form of sexual perversion, and is willing to grant this right reciprocally to others? And do not some people have special rights, for example, parents as contrasted with children? But these sorts of questions are beyond the scope of the Golden Rule, which has only to do with inculcating the proper moral dispositions, not with determining objectively what rights there are. Indirectly, however, the Golden Rule may have an influence in defining and corroborating certain very basic objective rights, for example, the rights to life, property and privacy (I claim a right to life for myself, and am also willing to grant it to others, etc.).

The proper subordination of means-to-end is another important aspect of rationality. And all the versions of the Golden Rule manifest this aspect insofar as they presume that each human being is an end-in-himself, on an equal level with others, and not to be subordinated to the ends or goals of any other. If and when someone breaks the Golden Rule (treats another individual in a way that he would not like to be treated, or does not grant the other a basic right which he claims for himself), he is subordinating that other person as a means to his own ends, failing to treat the other as an end-in-himself.

A final aspect of rationality envisaged by the Golden Rule is *universality*. In its pure logical form, universality means going beyond particulars (particular facts, particular instances, particular events) to a general idea which is applicable to all. The fact that human beings can formulate general concepts is thought by some to constitute the main claim to man's superiority over the other animals. But of course it is one thing to simply formulate a general concept of 'man' which can apply to Tom, Dick and Henriette, and to Asians, Africans and Europeans – and quite another to formulate a code of conduct which applies equally to all people. The latter ethical extension of man's ability for universalisation is embodied in all the various forms of the Golden Rule, which apply to 'others' without any explicit restrictions or exceptions. However, the Christian version seems to have some superiority in this respect. It is the only one that spells out (in the context of the 'Sermon on the Mount' in the Gospels) the applicability of the rule to all men, including even one's enemies. The other versions, taken in context and in their actual applicability, seem to apply primarily to the relevant culture or religious group, although they may not explicitly exclude other groups or cultures.

The Golden Rule has been praised by many moral philosophers and relatively few doubt its worth and cogency. As a subjective means for testing our intentions for adherence to basic standards of rationality, it is without peer in its comprehensiveness.

### 3(a) 2.2.   *Aristotle: Moderation and Sanity*

**A man is said to have or not to have self-control according as his reason has or has not the control, on the assumption that this**

[reason] is the man himself; and the things men have done on a rational principle are thought most properly their own acts and voluntary acts. That this [reason] is the man himself, then, or is so more than anything else, is plain, and also that the good man loves most this part of him.

Virtue . . . is a state of character concerned with choice, lying in a mean, i.e. the mean relative to us, this being determined by a rational principle. . . . It is a mean between two vices, that which depends on excess and that which depends on defect. . . .[28]

Richard Norman observes that Aristotle, along with a number of other distinguished philosophers, was guilty of simply justifying practices in his social milieu, rather than relying on rational argument.[29] In Aristotle's case, the most notable 'lapses' would be his assertions that slaves and women are subservient by nature, his contempt for manual work and insistence on the observance of social distinctions. But these are lapses of an objective sort – that is, an acceptance of certain objective norms as justified by nature, when there are really no grounds for their justification. Subjectively speaking, and within the parameters of his socio-cultural limitations, he was ahead of his time. At a time when most of his contemporaries were on the aesthetic/moral level, he was a pathfinder in the moral sphere. He was teaching that we should live in accord with that which is highest in us – the operations of reason. And the idea that reason should supersede passions, weaknesses and bad habits is one of the major catalysts which contributed to the eventual criticism and modification of some of the institutionalised injustices prevalent in the Western world.

A. E. Taylor compares Aristotle's 'doctrine of the mean' to the sort of reasoning process that a physician will go through in determining the proper treatment for a disease.[30] The comparison is particularly appropriate in light of the spread in Aristotle's era (4th century BC Greece) of the Hippocratean theory of medicine, which characterised health as a balance of opposites; and described the physician's role in terms of a judicious application of remedies, sometimes extreme, sometimes very conservative, in order to restore the natural healthy equilibrium or homeostasis of bodily fluids in the patient. So also the ethical life, in Aristotle's estimation, consists in maintaining the health of the soul by constantly aiming for a middle ground, a dynamic balance, between the various extremes to which our passions might lead us. This is by no means an exact mid-point or a mathematically calculable 'mean'. For example, since most people are inclined to eat too much rather than too little, the interests of rationality will lead us to eat a bit less than we desire, to keep us from succumbing to pleasure, the 'great deceiver'.[31] And similarly, since most people are inclined more to greed than to prodigality, we should try to be a little more generous than reason would require. The essential element in Aristotle's definition of virtue (see p. 49 above) is his emphasis on the determination of the mean by a *rational principle*. Virtue is determined by the constant use of reason to maintain or restore harmony in the various contingencies, relationships and environmental situations that arise, and not by some predetermined rule or measure. The mean in the case of virtue is truly a mean 'relative to us', a subjective mean. Only a continual effort at rational decision-making can keep one somewhere in the vicinity of the mean. The effort involved in moderating the excesses to which we may be temperamentally inclined does become less strenuous as we form habits of good conduct, and may become almost unnoticeable because of the pleasures that virtuous accomplishment brings to us.[32] But Stuart Hampshire's comparison of Aristotle's concept of ethical decision-making to the effortlessness and spontaneity of good manners[33] may be a misleading comparison. For the decisions involved, although bringing a certain pride and delight to the rational man, have to do on occasion with serious matters, violent passions and hard choices – which go considerably beyond the domain of good manners. Aristotle allows that there may be some who are endowed with the divine gift of 'natural virtue', and for them a gracious kind of virtuous activity, comparable to the good manners of sophisticated gentry, may be possible with less effort-expenditure.[34] But for the rest of us, whose passions have 'rough edges' which need smoothing down, presumably much deliberation and work will be necessary.

### 3(a) 2.3.   *Spinoza: Sublimation*

**An emotion which is a passion ceases to be a passion as soon as we form a clear and distinct idea of it. . . . In proportion, then, as**

we know an emotion better it is more within our control, and the less does the mind suffer from it.[35]

Everyone has the power, partly at least, if not absolutely, of understanding clearly and distinctly himself and his emotions, and consequently of bringing it to pass that he suffers less from them. We have therefore mainly to strive to acquire a clear and distinct knowledge as far as possible of each emotion, so that the mind may be led to pass from the emotion to think those things which it perceives clearly and distinctly, and with which it is entirely satisfied, and to strive also that the emotion may be separated from the thought of an external cause and connected with true thoughts.[36]

I should like to make some comparisons between Benedict Spinoza (1632–77) and Sigmund Freud; but before doing so I should make it clear that there are some important differences between the systematic context of Spinoza's doctrine and that of Freud. Freud was an atheist, Spinoza a pantheist; Freud's 'life instinct' (erotic impulse) and 'death instinct' (aggressivity) are elemental biological drives[37] while Spinoza's *conatus* or 'striving'[38] is an intrinsic drive to self-perfection implanted in every being; the proper channelling of human drives for Freud is on behalf of adaptation to one's social environment,[39] while the channelling of the human *conatus* for Spinoza is geared teleologically to certain higher stages of knowledge which bring about a union with the divine substance of the universe.[40]

These differences being adverted to, we are in a better position to appreciate the fact that there are also some important similarities. Although the term 'sublimation' was not used by Spinoza, he propounds a concept which bears the earmarks of the Freudian idea: sublimation, in Freud's psychoanalytic theory, involves the imposition of rationality by the ego upon the wayward and often anti-social impulses of the id. One cannot impose this rationality arbitrarily, but must understand and accommodate himself to the impulses as a rider accommodates himself to the powerful forces of the horse he is guiding.[41] So also Spinoza admonishes us that we must understand the emotions that the progression of our *conatus* subjects us to, and gradually, without trying to divest ourselves (if such a thing were possible) of our emotional nature, bring them under control at the same time as we are making use of them. We do

this by supplying for them the purposeful ideas which can give
them direction, and transform them from mere passive impulses
('passions') to actively engaged emotions in the service of
reason.

Another similarity between Spinoza and Freud is their
identification of mind with body. In Freud, the identification is from
a materialistic viewpoint. Although Freud speaks of a 'psyche',
there is nothing mystical or immaterial (no 'soul') connoted by this
term, and he makes it quite clear that he believes this psyche could
be resolved into certain ultimate material components, although he
himself is not particularly concerned with conducting such an
analysis. In Spinoza, the identification is from an idealistic-
pantheistic viewpoint. The mind and the body are just two aspects
of the same spiritual entity.[42] We constantly give evidence of the
metaphysical identity of reason and emotions by our power of
fusing emotions with the ideas of reason, thus bringing about a
sublimation of the emotions.

This ability to sublimate the emotions is shown, for example, if,
when I feel the passion of 'ambition' (that is, a desire to have people
live according to my desires), I then reflect on the way of properly
directing my emotion and sublimate it into 'piety' (that is, the
reasoned persuasion of others to live, as much as possible,
according to that which is best in them and in myself).[43] I may feel
the passion of glory, and, in order to direct this properly, make it
into an active emotion, by using my ingenuity to reflect on how best
to be worthy of the praise of others, and how to pursue it
legitimately, without detracting from the worth of other people.[44]
Or if I feel the passion of hatred, I may try to understand that my
enemy, like myself, is impelled by drives over which he ultimately
has no control, and I can set my mind to devising ways in which I
and my enemy may both contribute to the common good; and if that
is not possible I can resolve at least that I shall not waste my energy
in hostile thoughts and actions, and that as far as I am concerned, I
shall have no enemies.[45]

Both Spinoza and Freud advise the fullest possible awareness of
our 'passional' nature; but the sort of sublimation Spinoza advocates
is much more strenuous and much more active than that which
Freud recommends. We are urged, in Spinoza's system of values, to
use our reason not just to adapt to whatever social demands we are
faced with, but to give constant concrete proof of the belief we have
in the intrinsic rationality of our emotions.

## 3(a) 2.4.   *Adam Smith: Objectivity, Impartiality*

**We must become the impartial spectators of our own character and conduct. We must endeavour to view them with the eyes of other people, or as other people are likely to view them.**

**[If someone has acted contemptibly,] when he looks back upon [his action], and views it in the light in which the impartial spectator would view it, he finds that he can enter into none of the motives which influenced it. He is abashed and confounded at the thought of it, and necessarily feels a very high degree of that shame which he would be exposed to, if his actions should ever come to be generally known.**[46]

The Scottish philosopher Adam Smith (1723–90) is best known for his treatise on political economics, *The Wealth of Nations* (first published in 1776), the 'bible' of capitalism. In *The Wealth of Nations* we are presented with an argument for enlightened self-interest; the supposition is that if each person is freely allowed to pursue that which is to his profit, by the operation of some 'invisible hand' (the unseen social reverberations of the creation of wealth), all people will ultimately be benefited.

Smith's moral philosophy seems to stand in sharp contrast, almost in contradiction, to his economic philosophy. Instead of self-interest, the predominating motif is the 'sentiment' of sympathy. According to Smith, we have an innate ability, if we take the time to reflect on the situation of others, to reproduce by sympathy the feelings that these others have, or should have. And this gives us a basis for the determination of the worth or merit of various actions, and also, by a certain extension, for the determination of the merit of our own actions. This latter 'extension' allows us to become 'impartial spectators', as it were, of our own actions. For the sentiment of sympathy is like a concave object which, from another point of view, will appear convex. Just as it enables us to put ourselves 'in the shoes' of others, so also, by a reversal of perspective, it allows us to see ourselves as others see us. Any action of ours can be viewed and 'tested' in this way, if we simply take the time to make the 'impartial spectator' test. The result is, or should be, the attainment of a high degree of objectivity and impartiality – in a word, of rationality – with regard to our own actions.

Adam Smith never managed to explain or bridge the apparent gap between his ethical theory of sympathy and his economic theory of self-interest. We may be reasonably sure that this is *not* because he viewed the sphere of commerce and trade as a sphere in which ethics does not apply. In fact, we may presume that Smith never intended that his ethical theory should not apply to his theory of capitalism. And so, in line with those intentions, we should endeavour to visualise the classical Smithian capitalist working for profit-maximisation and yet at the same time being well-endowed with sentiments of sympathy, and willing to test his own decisions by viewing them as an 'impartial spectator'. If we have difficulty in fashioning such a composite idea, our difficulty may be due to a traditional, unconscionably sharp rift between the worlds of business and ethics – a situation which antedated Smith's theorising, and over which he himself could have little control.

### 3(a) 2.5.   Kant: Universality and Self-Consistency

> There is . . . but one categorical imperative, namely this: *Act only on that maxim whereby thou canst at the same time will that it should become a universal law. . . .* [Another way of expressing this same imperative would be:] *Act as if the maxim of thy action were to become by thy will a universal law of nature.*[47]

> Some actions are of such a character that their maxim cannot without contradiction be even *conceived* as a universal law of nature. . . . In others, this intrinsic impossibility is not found, but still it is impossible to *will* that their maxim should be raised to the universality of a law of nature, since such a will would contradict itself. . . . The former violate strict or rigorous (inflexible) duty; the latter only laxer (meritorious) duty.[48]

The famous 'categorical imperative' devised by the German philosopher, Immanuel Kant (1724–1804), is a test for two important aspects of rationality – universality and self-consistency (non-self-contradiction). The aspect of universality in our logical processes is not always connected with self-consistency. For example, if I universalised the bus-situation in my town, by saying 'all the buses in our town are yellow, charge fares, and carry passengers', this might be wrong if there was a red bus which carried cargo without charge; but explicit problems concerning self-consistency do not turn up in this sort of statement. If, however, I try to universalise some personal intention of mine, something I intend to do (a 'maxim' that I am prepared to put into practice), the issue of universality becomes intertwined with that of self-consistency. The same examples given by Kant, to illustrate the application of the categorical imperative, also illustrate the interconnection of universality and self-consistency: a man intends to borrow money with no intention of paying it back, and, applying Kant's test, tries to universalise this intent, that is, to will that everyone should borrow in this way. He cannot universalise it, because if everyone borrowed with no intent to pay, this would be inconsistent with the very idea of borrowing, and the institutions of lending and borrowing would be destroyed. Thus, Kant concludes, we have a 'strict duty' to borrow only with the intent of repaying. The same interconnection of universality and self-consistency is found in 'laxer duties', as the following example illustrates. A rich man intends to ignore the need of those who do not have enough for bare subsistence, and applies Kant's test, asking himself whether he could make his own hard-heartedness into a universal law. But of course he cannot, because he cannot self-consistently will that everyone would be hard-hearted to *him* (even a rich man has needs for affection, sympathy, recognition, etc.).

One who is familiar with the Golden Rule will immediately notice an apparent similarity between the Golden Rule and the categorical imperative, in so far as they both seem oriented to assuring universality and self-consistency in our moral behaviour; but there is at least one important difference: as Kant himself points out,[49] the Golden Rule does not envision duties to *oneself*, for example, the duty to preserve one's life and to cultivate one's talents. Thus it leaves out a very important sphere of duties. The other differences which Kant points out between the Golden Rule (Kant concentrates on the negative version: '*don't* do . . .') and the categorical imperative are not as clear-cut. First, he says that there are at least some 'strict duties' which the Golden Rule does not encompass. For example, a judge would not be able under the Golden Rule to perform his strict duty of punishing a criminal, if he did not wish to be so punished himself.[50] But with some rephrasing, the Golden Rule could be salvaged here: we could talk about a judge not ignoring the rights of the *victims* of the criminal, in a way that he would not like to be done to him if he himself were the *victim* of that criminal. Secondly, Kant asserts that there is a third difference between the two approaches: he says that the Golden Rule does not encompass, like the categorical imperative, the 'laxer duties', for example, benevolence; 'many a one would gladly consent that others should not benefit him, provided only that he might be excused from showing benevolence to them'.[51] But this example of Kant's seems to involve a misapplication of the negative version of the Golden Rule. This version of the Golden Rule would not say, 'don't excuse yourself from benefiting others unless you would consent that they not benefit you', but rather 'don't refuse to benefit others, if you don't wish others to *refuse* to benefit you'. In order to apply the Rule properly, we would have to rephrase part of Kant's paraphrase, thus: 'many a one would gladly consent that others should *refuse to benefit* him . . .'. This phrasing implies that the individual in question *needs*, and perhaps has even requested, the benefit from the other. And it is doubtful that he would gladly consent to their outright refusal.

It should be obvious from the discussion above that, in applying the categorical imperative as well as the Golden Rule, slight variations in *phrasing* can give rise to very different results. And some of the better known controversies regarding the validity or viability of the categorical imperative seem to hinge on contingencies of phrasing.

R. M. Hare gives the example of a hypothetical Nazi who would apply the Kantian test to his personal maxim, 'All Jews should be eliminated', and concludes that the Nazi would not be able to pass the test because he would not want this maxim to apply to himself if it should be discovered that he himself was of Jewish extraction. But Henry Veatch replies that the Nazi need only rephrase his maxim to something like this: 'All Jews should be eliminated except me (in case it should be discovered that I am Jewish'), and then the maxim could pass the Kantian test.[52] However, neither Hare nor Veatch are adhering to the proper form for the categorical imperative, which should begin with a personal maxim, for example, 'I intended to eliminate all Jews', and then be universalised to all men without exception, for example, 'All persons should dedicate themselves to eliminating Jews' – which presumably could not be a maxim for all persons, including those who, as in Hare's application, might fear that they are partly Jewish. However, it would seem that a dedicated and resourceful Nazi could still reformulate his maxim thus, 'I intend to eliminate all members of Jewish synagogues who have actually attended services for the last ten years', and successfully universalise this. In trying to justify an 'elimination' maxim, however, the Nazi would have to go into more detail about rationale and classification; for example, 'I wish to eliminate Jews as the group that has taken over all the most influential positions affecting the national economy and are adulterating our pure Aryan blood'. Presumably even our dedicated Nazi could not universalise this, unless *per impossibile* he was absolutely certain of having pure Aryan blood and of not appropriating any influential positions relinquished by the Jews.

One of the most controversial applications of the categorical imperative is one made by Kant himself, in response to Benjamin Constant, who ridiculed Kant for saying that the categorical imperative always requires that we tell the truth, even if we are asked by a murderer whether a certain innocent person, whom he wishes to murder, is in our house. Kant insists that lying would be wrong even in such a case, because it would be an offence against mankind generally, in so far as the one who lies helps to assure 'that declarations in general find no credit, and hence that all rights founded on contract should lose their force'.[53] Marcus Singer, on the other hand, argues that Kant is misapplying his own principles here. In order to have a complete and judicious application of the categorical imperative, says Singer, we have to give attention to all the relevant circumstances of the situation; but, in this case, 'Kant overlooked the fact that lying merely for one's own personal convenience, and lying in order to save the life of some innocent person, are two different sorts of actions, actions whose maxims are quite different'.[54] Thus if we are just willing to add the phrase, 'to save the life of an innocent person', to our maxim, we could universalise it. Another way of rephrasing the maxim to bring out the relevant circumstances more fully might be: 'I intend to tell a lie in those cases where the inquirer has no *right* to know that which he is inquiring about, and where I have no choice to remain silent.' Here again, this seems to be universalisable, although lying for one's personal convenience would still not be universalisable.

One of the most paradoxical applications of the categorical imperative would be in regard to Kant's own thesis that we should not take happiness as our goal in moral activity. Julius Ebbinghaus observes that if this thesis were tested as a maxim according to the rules set down by Kant, it would not be conformable to the categorical imperative, for we could quite easily and self-consistently universalise the maxim 'I intend to take happiness as my moral goal, as long as this intent doesn't infringe on the happiness of others'.[55] This would presumably be the most inconvenient conclusion of all for a Kantian, since it would seem to place him in the camp of his sworn enemy, the utilitarian! However, here again some rephrasing could drastically change the picture. I could add '. . . and as long as conformity to reason can be considered a species of happiness'. For the Kantian would balk at this latter condition, even though it might seem to *us* that for him (and for many people) conformity to reason through consistent universalisation of maxims is the *highest* form of happiness. Kant defines happiness as the 'fulfilment of all the inclinations', but does *not* include the desire for fulfilment of strict or laxer duties as an 'inclination whose fulfilment would lead to happiness'. And thus, if we wanted to adhere to the basic Kantian 'game rules', we would not be able to apply the categorical imperative in the way that Ebbinghaus does.

### 3(a) 2.6.   Kant: Means–End Proportionment

> **Rational beings . . . are called *persons*, because their very nature points them out as ends in themselves, that is, as something which must not be used merely as means, and so far therefore restricts freedom of action (and is an object of respect). . . . If then there is a supreme practical principle . . . the foundation of this principle is: *rational nature exists as an end in itself.* . . . Accordingly the practical imperative will be as follows: *So act as to treat humanity, whether in thine own person or in that of any other, in every case as an end withal, never as means only.*[56]**

Once one decides, in accordance with the categorical imperative (considered in section 2.5), to act in a universalisable and self-consistent manner, he must give some attention to the material objects of his activity, the sort of things he has to deal with. In particular, he has to consider the basic hierarchy with which reason is concerned – the proper relationship of means to end. This implies that he must decide in a general way what should be means and what should be ends. The result of this basic differentiation of means from ends leads to the 'second formulation' of the categorical imperative, just quoted, which presupposes universalisation and self-consistency, and attempts to make means-end co-ordination explicit, as an equally important function or aspect of reason.

In order to see how Kant arrived at this second formulation, we should begin by asking what sort of thing can and should be a means in human behaviour. If we try to answer this in a positive way, we end up with almost an infinite variety of means. But if we take a negative approach, trying to eliminate at the outset what could not possibly be a means, we find that we can easily come to agreement in eliminating the possibility that *persons* could be used *merely* as means. A person may be used partially as a means – for example, if I step on someone's shoulders to reach a second storey window. But it is unthinkable to use a person simply as a means to an end, the way one uses a pencil or a shoe or money. The latter sorts of things *are* used merely as means to our ends. (Kant seems to believe also that animals, not being rational beings, can be used as mere means to an end; but this seems to be a more ambiguous case, since at least the higher animals approximate rationality.) And so we end up with the following results of the first phase of our inquiry: an almost infinite number of things, possibly animals also, can be used as means; but persons can never be used as *mere* means.

Having considered the problem of means, we turn now to the question of ends: what is the proper end or goal of human activity? Because of Kant's peculiar characterisation of happiness (as something which can never be the goal of moral choices), he cannot, like Aristotle, present us with happiness as a kind of self-evident end. In fact, a moral agent, in making his choices, can in Kant's estimation have no end outside himself. But he can and does take himself (his rational nature, his personality) as his end. He takes his rational nature as his 'end', in the sense that it is something he is dedicated to maintaining and fostering. And since he does this in his own case, he is constrained by his universal orientation and self-consistency (entailed by the first formulation of the categorical imperative) to do the same with respect to others, that is, to take the rational nature of other people also as an 'end' in the above sense.[57] D. D. Raphael perceives a theoretical basis for utilitarianism in such statements, in so far as the 'respect for persons' which Kant enjoins would imply a desire for, and an intention to promote, the happiness of others – the fundamental thrust of utilitarianism.[58] But this interpretation would be to take Kant beyond his intended limits. The 'respect for persons' enjoined by Kant is a moral deference to others in so far as these others have moral capacities like ourselves. Any happiness that would result to us or to them from our strictly moral interrelationships would be a mere contingency, not explicitly intended or provided for. The nature of Kant's second formulation as a subjective 'test' also contraindicates any effective parallelism with utilitarianism. While classical utilitarianism purports to offer an objective norm for moral behaviour, namely, the quantity and/or intensity of concrete enjoyable and beneficial consequences that we can produce, Kant's second formulation is simply a subjective means for testing the quality of our basic orientation in relating to ourselves and others.

The *strictest* duties entailed from the second 'means-to-end' formulation of the categorical imperative have to do with its negative injunction not to use ourselves or others as mere means. Thus, to use Kant's examples, we are strictly enjoined not to use our own death in suicide as a means to escape from pain, and not to use another's misinformation through our lying promise as a means to obtaining a loan from him.[59] The 'laxer' duties are derived from the other *positive* injunction to take our own or others' rational nature as an end to preserve and foster. Thus, for example, we have a duty to foster the various capabilities which we as a person have, but it is not necessary to be doing this at all times, or with constant attention only to the highest capabilities; and we have a duty to promote the rational objectives of others, although it is not necessary to do this for everyone, at all times, or to the highest degree.[60]

Alasdair MacIntyre has characterised the categorical imperative and other such deontological statements as the 'ghost' of the ancient-medieval notion of a divine law.[61] This observation seems to be especially true of the first formulation – an extraordinary attempt to lay down some absolute guidelines derived from pure reason alone, not from any supernatural revelation. With regard to the second formulation of the categorical imperative, however, it would seem that the most appropriate analogy would be not with divine law but with the Christian concept of man as having an immortal soul which makes him the image of God, and leads him to respect and revere that same image in other humans. Kant's eighteenth-century Enlightenment version of this, *sans* revelation, is the concept of the rational being, fully conscious of the power and dignity of rationality in himself and others, and prepared to act in a way which is consonant with that consciousness.

### 3(a) 3.   Procedures for Ascertaining/Inculating Self-Consciousness

As has already been indicated, there are long-standing disputes among philosophers as to whether there is some outstanding quality or excellence distinguishing human beings from other animals, and as to what this might be. There are some who have argued that man has no power of self-determination; others who have maintained that man's reason is just a more sophisticated version of capacities found in other animals. In particular, ongoing experiments with some of the higher mammals have indicated that animals may indeed have rational abilities such as the power of universalisation or the ability to apply means to ends.[62] If we were looking for a distinguishing characteristic not only uniquely utilised by men, but also unique to men, perhaps, as I have argued elsewhere,[63] self-consciousness would be the closest approximation to such a characteristic.

In a wide sense, it might be said that all the moral theories we have discussed to this point have been oriented towards self-consciousness. But there are some ethical approaches which are geared more explicitly to the inculcation of self-consciousness, and according to which the habit and practice of self-reflection constitutes the primary and indispensable subjective springboard for moral activity. The first position we will consider – that of Socrates (470–399 BC) – is the catalyst which first set in motion the type of thinking which is to be found in the history of ethical theorising in the Western world. This initial catalyst is not a 'theory' in the strict sense, but more properly an approach or method. It is not only historically prior to the other ethical theories, but may be considered basic to all ethical theorising, as well as to practical moral activity.

### 3(a) 3.1.   *Socrates: Critical Self-Knowledge*

> [Socrates:] When I was young . . . I had a prodigous desire to know that department of philosophy which is called the investigation of nature; to know the causes of things, and why a thing is and is created or destroyed appeared to me to be a lofty profession. . . . I heard someone reading, as he said, from a book of Anaxagoras, that mind was the disposer and cause of all, and I was delighted at this notion. . . . How grievously was I

disappointed! As I proceeded, I found my philosopher
altogether forsaking mind or any other principle of order, but
having recourse to air, and ether, and water, and other
eccentricities. . . . I thought that as I had failed in the
contemplation of true existence . . . I had better have recourse to
the world of mind and seek there the truth of existence.[64]

Daily to discourse about virtue . . . is the greatest good of man,
and . . . the unexamined life is not worth living.[65]

As [Socrates] could not always have at hand one to argue
against his principles or to be argued against in turn, he used to
argue with and examine himself, and he was always treating at
least some one subject in a practical way.[66]

Offhand, Socrates (as depicted by Plato) presents us with an image
which seems exactly the obverse of modern man: Socrates, after
studying the various conflicting theories about the nature and origin
of the physical universe, despaired of ever discovering the truth
about the external world, and decided to investigate an area where
he could have greater certainty of discovering the truth, namely, the
inner world of human values. We, in contrast, faced with many
different conflicting theories about human values, might tend to
look with relief to the science of physics as an area where there is a
relative consensus about the essential aspects of the origin and
nature of the universe (the 'big bang theory', the law of entropy, the
expanding universe, the speed of light, etc.). Some modern
philosophers are even impatient of talk about the 'inner' man and
his values. Those who tolerate this talk, or even welcome it, may still
have to admit candidly that questions about the inner nature or
mechanisms of consciousness and its value-formations cannot be
answered with a degree of clarity or exactitude even faintly
resembling the enviable certitude of the physical cosmologists.

If Socrates were aware of this situation, he would find it strange
that anyone could have more certitude about the external world
than about the inner psyche. He would object that the inner world is
close at hand, much closer than the external world; all we need do,
he would say, is attend to it, examine it carefully, and work out some
conclusions, preferably in unison with others who might join us in
examining the inner values that we share. In short, the optimism of
Socrates is due to the emphasis he placed on the power of

consciousnesses to examine themselves, that is, on the power of self-consciousness. (Those extreme extroverts for whom 'self-consciousness' is only a synonym for acute shyness or neuroticism may be excused if they prefer to concentrate their attention on the external world.)

The external questioning process ('cross-examination') that Socrates is noted for, is, then, just a continuation and extension of the inner questioning process of an extraordinarily self-reflective individual. The enterprise that he and his fellow questioners entered upon set the standard for Western philosophy, to such an extent that everything prior to this enterprise is called 'pre-Socratic'. It is perhaps important and even indispensable that we should recall, from time to time, that ethics began with this constant questioning process, this continual examination and reassessment of values. This same process, on the individual level, is conscience.

The French language can help to illuminate this point. In French, the word for 'consciousness', *la conscience*, is the same as the word for 'conscience'. Presumably it would be easier for a Frenchman than for an English-speaking person to see conscience as a function of self-consciousness. But we all need to make this connection if we are to avoid portraying conscience as a set of ready-made values or attitudes.

Many moral people, even many moral philosophers, would look upon the constant self-questioning of a Socrates as unsatisfying and disturbing. They might even frame their objections in terms of the goal of happiness: wouldn't one be happier living an unexamined life? A Socrates, they would surmise, must almost certainly be an essentially unhappy person, one at odds with himself.

On the other hand, could a human being be happy if he didn't know he was happy? It is hard to conceptualise a pure, unreflective ('first-order') happiness. For humans, at least for human beings like Socrates, the greatest happiness consists in knowing that they are happy, and why, and whether and how the happiness is justified. One could carry this reflective process to extremes, of course. But the latter 'second-order' happiness is of the highest degree, simply because it brings into operation the highest operations of consciousness. Socrates shows us that these highest operations consist in discovery, discrimination, co-ordination and activation of our greatest human potentialities, giving rise to acts of virtue.

Socrates as a moral philosopher is perhaps best compared to the artist or athlete who is constantly engaged in re-evaluation and

self-criticism, with a view to perfecting his prowess and
performance in his specific art or profession. But Socrates was
interested in a much more general art, the art of living, which also
requires not only practice but constant re-evaluation if one is to do it
well.

Since we have no reliable writings from Socrates, and our
knowledge of him is thus completely dependent on Plato's
imaginative dramatisations of Socrates' character, it is hard to get at
the 'real' Socrates. It has appeared to some students of Plato's
dialogues that Socrates rarely came to any definite conclusions; they
might even allege (unkindly) that this indefiniteness is the reason
Socrates never wrote out his ideas, and ask (equally unkindly)
whether he might not have attained a greater degree of certitude if
he had stuck with his study of cosmological theories. But this would
be inaccurate as well as unkind. Socrates did indeed come to quite a
few conclusions, although they were largely negative in nature. He,
along with his interlocutors, concludes in Plato's *Republic*, for
example, that justice is not the rule of the stronger; in the *Euthyphro*
that piety is not 'bringing all wrongdoers to justice'; in the *Meno*,
that virtue is neither given by nature nor essentially connected with
knowledge; in the *Lysis* that friendship does not rely solely on the
attraction of 'like to like'; in the *Laches*, that courage does not consist
in persistence, etc. Socrates even comes to some occasional tentative
positive conclusions. But these latter are perhaps not his most
important findings. Is it possible that, as seems to be the case with
Socrates, ethics can be more successful in coming up with definite
conclusions of a negative nature, than with definitive positive rules?
This possibility will be discussed in Chapter 5.

### 3(a) 3.2.   *Kierkegaard: Knowledge and Choice of One's Self*

> **Ethics says that it is the significance of life and of reality that
> every man become revealed. . . . The aestheticist, on the
> contrary, . . . remains constantly concealed. . . . But this thing
> of playing hide and seek always avenges itself, and of course it
> does so by the fact that one becomes enigmatical to oneself.[67]**

> **The self which the [ethical] individual knows is at once the
> actual self and the ideal self which the individual has outside
> himself as the picture in likeness to which he has to form himself**

and which, on the other hand, he nevertheless has in him since it is the self.[68]

> At the instant of choice [the ethical individual] is at the conclusion, for he concludes himself in a unity, and yet the same instant he is at the beginning, for he chooses himself freely. As product [of his circumstances] he is pressed into the forms of reality; in the choice he makes himself elastic, transforming all the outwardness into inwardness. This concretion is the reality of the individual, . . . his task.[69]

The existentialist Søren Kierkegaard (1813–55) makes a sharp distinction between the 'aesthetic' sphere of existence, in which an individual is attuned to avoiding serious reflection and interested only in taking advantage of the opportunities offered him for fulfilling his inclinations; and the 'ethical' sphere, in which the individual comes to grips reflectively with his 'ideal' self, in such a way that the direction and quality of his life is substantially changed.

The 'ideal self' in Kierkegaard's philosophy is meant to replace universals such as Kant's 'categorical imperative', which Kierkegaard considered to be overly abstract. The ideal self *is* a universal, but a *concrete* universal that springs from a reflective grasp of our own talents, capabilities, background and environment. Through a process of introspection we begin to catch a glimpse of our ideal self – not an unreal ideal, or a pure 'ought', to which we can only look up in guilt or admiration – but a realisable ideal uniquely possible to our own individual personality. Having caught this glimpse, it is possible either to welcome or to flee from the self-consciousness which it makes possible to us.

If one welcomes this state of self-consciousness and enters into the 'transcendence' of the ethical sphere, it is very difficult to account for the 'leap' that has taken place.[70] One way of accounting for the leap might be to make an analogy with lying: it seems that lying about serious matters can bring about a state of physiological distress or disharmony in many people (not pathological liars). Professional polygraphists claim that this state can be measured with some accuracy by a polygraph (lie-detector) test which analyses and co-ordinates data concerning blood pressure, respiration, pulse, galvanic skin response, voice patterns, etc., when a subject is tested for truth-telling. Whether or not accurate measurement is possible, let us presume that lying does cause a state of emotional distress in sensitive individuals. So also, when a sufficiently sensitive individual has caught a glimpse of his ideal self and fails, because of laziness, distractions or external obstacles, to take any steps to choose that self – that is, to 'choose himself' and actualise himself – he is caught up in an inner lie, a denial of the truth about .himself, which can bring about a state of inner spiritual distress, even despair. This inner distress in an optimistic scenario may be the springboard to positive ethical existence, in which one takes himself as his lifelong 'task'. The prerequisites for attaining this latter state are a certain inwardness which will enable the individual to apprehend his ideal self, a certain honesty to himself about this apprehension, and a certain courage in implementing the apprehension.

When one with full interiority and self-consciousness has taken himself as his 'task' – to use Kierkegaard's terminology – the paradoxical result should be a new-found freedom from rules and laws. One who is fully self-conscious will naturally and spontaneously do what is right without needing to be regulated by a multiplicity of external rules and laws. And in a society where others are also acting on a similar basis of self-consciousness, the mutual respect that results will assure each individual of explicit ethical recognition from others. When others in society are not so motivated, the ethical individual may expect some unavoidable external conflicts due to the misunderstandings of those others. But he or she will to a great extent have transcended the state of *internal* conflict. And this, to the ethical sort of individual, is the most important attainment, the most fundamental task.

As may be surmised, Kierkegaard's notion of ethical self-consciousness is not something that would be explicitly applicable to all the practical decisions that one makes in life. The inward intensity that he advocates could be summoned up only now and then, under favourable conditions, even by habitually reflective individuals. Kierkegaard himself indicates that the practical results of the choice of self will only become evident when one is involved in making major life choices. The two examples which Kierkegaard gives are: the choice of a career[71] and the choice of a spouse.[72] It is such long-range decisions that will be especially influenced by the character of the 'choice of self' that we have made. Once these long-range decisions are made, their implementation requires innumerable short-range choices which branch off quite logically from a few pivotal choices. However, even if the choice of self could not be explicitly connected with any specific practical long-range or short-range choices, it would still be the one necessary and sufficient condition for living an ethical, that is, a fully self-conscious, life.

### 3(a) 4. A Procedure for Ascertaining/Promoting Advanced Social Consciousness: Kant's 'Kingdom of Ends'

To whatever laws any rational being may be subject, he being an end in himself must be able to regard himself as also legislating universally in respect of these same laws, since it is just this fitness of his maxims for universal legislation that distinguishes him as an end in himself; also it follows that this implies his dignity (prerogative) above all mere physical beings, that he must always take his maxims from the point of view which regards himself, and likewise every other rational being, as lawgiving beings (on which account they are called persons). In this way a world of rational beings (*mundus intelligibilis*) is possible as a kingdom of ends, and this by virtue of the legislation proper to all persons as members. Therefore, *every rational being must so act as if he were by his maxims in every case a legislating member in the universal kingdom of ends.*[73]

In intimating that Kant's third formulation of the 'categorical imperative' is a procedure for inculcating 'social consciousness', I need first to make three disclaimers: (a) the notion of a social consciousness in Kant is not comparable to that of anthropologists or psychologists who speak of man's social 'instinct' or 'social propensity' as something shared with other animals, although possessed to a greater degree by humans; (b) Kant would not agree with John Dewey, Kurt Baier and other moralists, who (as mentioned above[74]) view morality as exclusively social; and (c) Kant is not even asserting that morality 'involves' certain social relations, but only that an ultimate and definitive means for assuring the validity of our personal morality is to test our specific individual intents or purposes against the broad background of a very sophisticated conception of social relations.

A comparison was made earlier,[75] between the first two formulations of the categorical imperative and certain pivotal concepts in the Christian religion. If the first formulation is analogous to the Christian concept of a divine law, and the second

formulation to the Christian idea of the eternal worth of the
individual soul, this third formulation is quite clearly an attempt to
develop on the basis of purely rational principles something
analogous to the Christian notion of the 'Kingdom of God', which
some claim to be the pivotal and indispensable doctrine of
Christianity.[76] As Paton observes, in using the German word *Reich*,
Kant seems to be following the lead of German translators of the
New Testament who translated the Greek, *Basileia*, by *Reich* in the
phrase, *Das Reich Gottes* ('The Kingdom of God'), although they
might have used the more specific (but more political) term,
*Königreich*.[77] And of the various Christian interpretations of 'The
Kingdom of God', Kant seems to have definitely had in mind the
Pauline idea of the 'Mystical Body of Christ' – a concept to which
Kant makes specific reference towards the end of his *Critique of Pure
Reason*, where he gives an initial brief sketch of the moral
implications entailed by his critical theory.[78] The Pauline idea,
which is also the source of many fundamental ethical notions in St
Paul's theology, portrays a social-spiritual organism in which each
individual member has specific functions, all contributing to
harmonious, unified activity of the whole, under the headship of
Christ.[79] So also Kant envisions an ideal social organism in which
each unique and indispensable participant would be legislating
universally and acting with respect for, and in consonance with, all
other participants, under the ultimate direction of a supreme
sovereign Lawgiver, who himself would be beyond the laws of
nature and the exigencies of human duty.[80]

It is worth noting that, while Kant offers a variety of examples for
the first two formulations of the categorical imperative, he offers no
specific *examples* to illustrate the application of this third
formulation. This is partly due to the fact that the third formulation
is meant to be a composite or synthesis of the other two formulations
(and of their possible applications), but also partly due to the fact
that the third formulation is not just a general procedure or rule, but
a political-moral idea, an overarching ideal which is meant to serve
as a criterion both for *our* relations to society and also for the validity
of the complexus of relations in which our *society* is involved. If we
want a 'practical application' of the ideal of a 'kingdom of ends', we
would do well to look to Kant's political philosophy, an outstanding
feature of which was the ideal of an international federation of
republics made up of free and independent people joined in
commitment to personal rights and the rule of law.[81] This ideal was

considered utopian in Kant's time, and is still considered by many to be practically unattainable, in spite of the possible structural beginnings made available to mankind by the United Nations Organization. But whether or not the ideal is ever practically implemented, in the Kantian framework it can be regarded as a means for testing one's moral fibre and the quality of one's political/moral allegiances.

## 3(b) ATTEMPTS TO ASCERTAIN AND/OR PROMOTE OBJECTIVE NORMS TO WHICH HUMAN BEHAVIOUR SHOULD CORRESPOND

Objective moral norms, as indicated already,[82] are meant to supply an absolute framework, in the light of which the lesser aesthetic/ moral objective norms may be superseded or reinterpreted. In particular, the relativistic aesthetic/moral social norms are superseded by some more comprehensive aspects of society, or even by mankind itself, as supplying the ultimate framework; and attempts are made to subordinate the more provincial scientific norms of human behaviour (sociobiology and the psychology of moral development were adduced above as contemporary examples) to some more stable and perennial norms derived from the teleology of human nature itself, philosophically interpreted. Of the moral theories that follow, some will emphasise the necessity for broader social norms, some will emphasise the necessity of looking to nature itself for our norms, and some will, within the parameters of their interpretation of 'society' and 'nature' give rather equal emphasis to both necessities.

### 3(b) 1.  Natural Law Theories

Erik Wolf has shown that, because of the multiple connotations of 'nature' and 'law', and the multiplicity of combinations possible among these connotations, there are 120 possible meanings of 'natural law'; and Ernst Bloch, following Spiegelberg, goes on to show how even in a single author the concept of a 'natural law' may be employed in a multiplicity of senses.[83] Thus the term 'natural law' is not a general classification which neatly sums up a certain class of theories, but an oversized 'umbrella' term which encompasses within its ambit theories about eternal ideas in the mind of God, about cosmic regularities and rhythms, about common-denominator customs prevailing among all men, about some 'state of nature' of primitive man, about the 'natural' (logical, non-self-contradictory) use of reason, and so forth. We will concentrate here only on a few pivotal classical natural law theories (or variations in natural law theory) in the history of Western philosophy – namely, Stoicism, Thomistic natural law theory, and the natural law theory of Hugo Grotius.

All three of these theories purport to find, from a study of nature in general and human nature in particular, some evidence regarding general norms which are (or ought to be – the distinction between 'is' and 'ought' is not remarkable in these theories) applicable to all persons at all times and in all places. These immutable laws are thought to be so basic that they can provide an unfailing criterion according to which all subsidiary laws – civil, criminal and international, as well as all other written or unwritten laws – are to be judged. Needless to say, natural law theories are bolstered best by stable theories of nature – 'stable' both in the sense that the theories are not rapidly changing, and also in the sense that nature itself is not thought to be in the process of rapid and unpredictable linear change. It is, as we shall see, much more difficult to champion a consistent and comprehensive traditional 'natural law' theory in modern times, in which the universe, culture, and even human nature are thought to be subject to evolution, and in which the theories themselves are demonstrated by metatheorists (such as Thomas Kuhn) to be evolving.

### 3(b) 1.1.   Stoicism

> **There is in fact a true law – namely, right reason – which is in accordance with nature, applies to all men, and is unchangeable and eternal. By its commands this law summons men to the performance of their duties; by its prohibitions it restrains them from doing wrong. Its commands and prohibitions always influence good men, but are without effect upon the bad. . . . [This law] will not lay down one rule at Rome and another at Athens, nor will it be one rule today and another tomorrow. But there will be one law, eternal and unchangeable, binding at all times upon all people; and there will be, as it were, one common master and ruler of men, namely God, who is the author of this law, its interpreter, and its sponsor. The man who will not obey**

it will abandon his better self, and, in denying the true nature of a man, will thereby suffer the severest of penalties, though he has escaped all the other consequences which men call punishment.

Cicero, *De Re Publica*[84]

Do not look around you to discover other men's ruling principles, but look straight to this, to what nature leads you, and your own nature through the acts which must be done by you. But every being ought to do that which is according to its constitution; and all other things have been constituted for the sake of rational beings, just as among irrational things the inferior for the sake of the superior, but the rational for the sake of one another.

Marcus Aurelius (121–80 AD)[85]

Never, when asked one's country, [should you answer], 'I am an Athenian or a Corinthian,' but 'I am a citizen of the world'. . . . He that has grasped the administration of the World, who has learned that this Community, which consists of God and men, is the foremost and mightiest and most comprehensive of all – why should such a one not call himself a citizen of the world?

Epictetus (50–138 AD)[86]

The Stoic philosophy, which had some distant Greek roots, matured and flourished under the auspices of Roman culture in the first two centuries of the Christian era. In the acme of its development, Stoicism presents a sharp contrast to the provincialism of the Greek city-state and the rather élitist views of human nature entertained by the relatively small number of fortunate Greek citizens who, in their heyday, looked upon the rest of the world as 'barbarians'.

External circumstances helped to further and finalise the cosmopolitanism of late Stoicism: the emergence of the new Roman Empire, destined to encompass the greater part of the then-known world, was a catalyst to the creation of a new kind of citizen who could look beyond local and even national allegiances to a world social order, of which he and his fellow citizens were not insignificant participants. And further, the prevalence of a monistic cosmology, according to which God or the Logos was the life-giving soul of the eternally recurring cycles of the cosmic order, offered a model of ideal harmony after which human affairs might be conscientiously and consistently patterned.

Stoicism, as a 'natural law' theory, emphasises conformity to nature, including human nature, which is the highest and clearest manifestation of the general rationality of nature; but it also emphasises, perhaps more than any other 'natural law' theory, a consciousness of a world social order, and a conformity to certain norms articulated by 'mankind' in general.

Just what specific standards of behaviour are entailed by Stoic conformity to nature and to world citizenship? Certainly their idea of absolute human equality, and of the consequent absolute immorality of slavery, was amazingly ahead of the times, and has had some of the farthest-reaching implications. It is significant that two of the best-known Stoics – Epictetus and Marcus Aurelius – were a slave and an emperor, respectively. Stoicism was a philosophy which cut across all distinctions of class, and it was implicitly oriented towards abolishing inequality and discrimination. The still recent abolition of the last vestiges of legalised bond-service during the 1960s and 1970s is perhaps one of the ultimate consequences of a vision first articulated by Stoicism (slavery still is practised in certain countries, but without the protective umbrella of legality).

This vision of human equality was interconnected in Stoicism with the concomitant ideal of a harmonious ecumenical social order – an ideal that has dimmed somewhat over the centuries, with the rise of the nation-state and modern conceptions of the 'balance of power', but may possibly be retrievable.

More specific applications of Stoic principles in the legal sphere led to the justification of the right of self-defence; and to a movement away from retributive (as contrasted with deterrent) punishment, and especially away from frequent recourse to capital punishment. The stoic idea of 'conformity to nature' was spelled out in a practical way by the laws against incest included in the second-century *Institutiones* of the jurist known as 'Gaius'.

One indirect effect of Stoicism, in conjunction with pre-establishment Roman Christianity, was the gradual relaxation of the grip of positive laws and political institutions, which were now subjected to criticism on the basis of natural, universal and/or eternal criteria. From the vantage point of modern liberal democratic theory, an essential feature of which is the power to critically re-examine laws and institutions, the latter effect may be seen as an indisputable long-range benefit.

*3(b) 1.2.   Thomistic Natural Law*

> The light of natural reason, by which we discern what is good and evil, is nothing other than the impression of divine light in us. And so it is clear that the natural law is just a participation by the rational creature in the eternal. . . . [This] natural law, as regards its primary common principles, is the same among all men, in respect to its validity and knowability.
>
> Thomas Aquinas, *Summa theologiae*, I–II, 91,2; 94,4

> The various precepts of the natural law are ordered among themselves in the way that our natural inclinations are ordered among themselves: First of all man has an inclination (shared with all other substances) towards what is good according to the nature which he shares with all substances; that is, insofar as each substance is oriented towards the preservation of its existence according to its specific nature. And in correspondence with this inclination, everything by means of which human life is preserved, and by means of which what is contrary to this preservation is prevented, pertains to the natural law. Secondly man has an inclination to certain special things in accord with the nature which he shares with the other animals. And thus those things 'which nature teaches to all animals' are said to belong to the natural law – for example the mating of male and female, the education of their progeny, and so forth. Thirdly, man has an inclination to the good which is in correspondence to a rational nature, which is his special attribute: for example, the natural inclination towards the knowledge of the truth about God, and towards social life. And thus, things which are associated with this rational inclination are also pertinent to the natural law: resulting, for example, in the law that a human being should avoid ignorance, should not offend those with whom he ought to associate, etc.
>
> *Ibid.*, 94,2

In Chapter 2 we saw that St Thomas Aquinas apparently developed the idea of a *vis cogitativa* out of some relatively inchoate ideas in

Aristotle's *Nicomachean Ethics* and *De Anima*.[87] Similarly, Aquinas
seems to have derived the notion of natural law at least partially out
of some suggestions in Aristotle's *Rhetoric* and *Nicomachean Ethics*[88]
concerning a law superseding various positive laws. (Although
Aquinas was familiar with the tenets of Stoicism, he does not use
Stoicism as the basis for his theory of natural law.) In Aquinas the
Aristotelian idea of a natural law, buttressed by Aristotelian
psychology, is also combined with the Augustinian idea of an
eternal law[89] and Judaeo-Christian scriptural teachings concerning
a law which applies to all people.[90] Thomistic 'natural law' is an
important (but not necessarily the *most* important) ethical principle
in the great medieval Aristotelian–Christian synthesis for which
Aquinas is noted.

Aquinas's theory of natural law can be contrasted with the Stoic
theory in two important respects:

3(b) 1.21.   Aquinas's theory is even more *specific* about what the
natural law requires. The natural law entails, among other things,
the law of self-preservation; the duty of the species (not necessarily
the individual) to propagate itself; the proper education of children;
self-education; communal co-operation; and the avoidance of
unnecessary offence to others.[91] It also prohibits the killing of
innocent people, stealing, polyandry and adultery.[92]

3(b) 1.22.   The Thomistic theory is also less *cosmopolitan* than the
Stoic theory. It does not envision a universal social order in which all
men are equal participants. Indeed, the Thomistic emphasis is not
so much on social ideals as on the Aristotelian concept of nature,
human nature particularly, and on the social conclusions which can
be derived logically in a rather immediate way from this concept. No
doubt Aristotle's *Politics*, which did not go beyond the nation-state
or even the city-state to some more ecumenical political-social ideal,
and which presented an attractive political philosophy in the highly
decentralised post-Holy-Roman-Empire medieval feudal society,
was in the background of Aquinas's thinking and may have
provided some ultimate parameters for his speculation.

From the vantage point of twentieth-century ethics and moral
theology, we can perceive other ways in which the Thomistic
natural law theory may have been hampered by some of its

Aristotelian presuppositions, leading to some strange (from the contemporary viewpoint) inversions of values. For example:

3(b) 1.23.   The Aristotelian idea of natural teleology, as applied to human sexual functions, leads Aquinas to the conclusion that masturbation and homosexuality are more serious sexual offences than rape, since they are more 'unnatural' (that is, do not involve ordinary intercourse between male and female).[93]

3(b) 1.24.   Likewise, the Aristotelian social philosophy according to which some men are 'natural' slaves,[94] may have had some influence on St Thomas's own acceptance of slavery.[95] And in view of the fact that Thomism became the official theology/philosophy of the Catholic Church, it is possible that the intermittent official acceptance of slavery by the Church until the latter part of the nineteenth century[96] may be similarly attributable to the fact that Aristotle, who was taken as an authority in natural law, did not condemn slavery, and actually condoned it.

If one were to compare the Thomistic and the Stoic versions of natural law just on the basis of their prescience (or lack of it) concerning slavery, he might conclude that the Stoic version is superior. However, it must be kept in mind that St Thomas himself made a distinction between basic precepts of the natural law, and specific applications, in which error may be involved. For instance (to use one of St Thomas's own examples) the barbarian German tribes generally approved of highway robbery, thus making a faulty 'application' of the natural law 'due to regrettable customs' (*ex mala consuetudine*); and to his credit, Aquinas, although he does cite with approval Aristotle's arguments in ɪ *Politics* justifying slavery, states that slavery is not strictly part of the natural law, but one of the derivative applications of 'natural justice'.[97]

Certainly if one confines himself to the general principles enunciated above (in paragraph 1.21), he will find nothing particularly objectionable, although he may not agree with Aquinas concerning the way that these principles are necessarily connected with 'nature'. And if we in the 'nuclear' era were to give serious consideration to the first and most basic principle of the natural law – that of self-preservation – we might even conclude that the discovery of *non-faulty* applications of such a principle may be the most important contemporary moral challenge for mankind.

### 3(b) 1.3.   The Empirical Natural Law

> That anything is or is not a part of nature may be proved by two
> kinds of argument, *a priori* and *a posteriori*, the former a more
> subtle method and the latter more popular. We are using the *a
> priori* method when we show the necessary agreement or
> disagreement of a thing with a reasonable and social nature; the *a
> posteriori* when, without absolute certainty but yet on strong
> probability, we infer that a thing is part of the law of nature
> which is accepted as such among all, or at least among all the
> more civilized nations. For a universal effect demands a
> universal cause. And the cause for so universal an opinion can
> scarcely be anything but the common sense, as it is called, of
> mankind.
>
> Hugo Grotius (1583–1645)[98]

In order to appreciate some of the subtle changes that were
introduced into 'natural law' theory in the seventeenth and
eighteenth centuries, by philosophers and jurists such as Grotius,
Pufendorf, Montesquieu and others, we should take into
consideration: (a) the development of a new, experimentally
oriented approach to science, exemplified by Galileo and Bacon; (b)
the explorations and discoveries of Columbus, Dias, Coronado, Da
Gama and others which had altered the parameters of the European
ideas of human nature and society; and (c) the Thirty Years' War and
other wars which racked Europe and raised questions as to whether
there might not be some common human values which could be
appealed to, to mitigate the increasing lawlessness. In view of these
challenges, the traditional natural law theories, which were
deduced *a priori* (that is, non-empirically) from certain abstract and
sometimes questionable philosophical principles began to seem
unsatisfactory, and the question began to be posed: why not
examine what we now know about other peoples and cultures, and
the values and laws that the most important of them have in
common, and thus bolster our 'natural law' theory with empirical *a
posteriori* evidence acceptable even to the most sceptical?

Long before the fifteenth century the Stoic jurist Gaius had
spoken about a *jus gentium*, the 'law of nations', a sort of repository
of all that is rational in the existing customs and laws of nations. But
Grotius wanted to take this idea one step further: our knowledge of
the 'law of nations', now greatly expanded by exploration and

discovery, could be used as an empirical laboratory in which we might discover the basic tenets of the natural law. What better way to establish the basic tenets of the natural law than to actually examine the numerous ways that human nature manifests itself, and the various values that men really do hold in common? Grotius himself did not advocate any radical break with tradition. He allowed for a 'pure philosophical' *a priori* derivation of the natural law. But he proposed to supplement and corroborate this derivation through empirical means. Others after him would make the more radical break with tradition.

The practical conclusions that Grotius came to with regard to the specific tenets of the natural law are in some ways similar, and in some ways different than in the case of previous 'natural law' theories. He held with Aristotle that equity and justice were important aspects of the natural law, with the Stoics that the recognition of human equality was of the utmost importance, and with the Thomists that parental responsibility and marital fidelity were laws of nature. He differed somewhat from previous natural law theorists in the greater emphasis he placed on the keeping of promises, which he considered to be the cornerstone of natural law. This latter emphasis is easily understood if one realises that Grotius was looking primarily for a firm foundation for international relations, the keeping of treaties, and the prevention of wars. In the sphere of international relations, the keeping of promises is no doubt the most relevant and important 'natural law'.

As was indicated above, others after Grotius began to emphasise more strongly, or even exclusively, the empirical aspects of natural law. This tendency led to two extreme results.

3(b) 1.31.   To some it occurred that the best way to determine the 'law of nature' for man would be to investigate, if possible, the condition of man in the natural state, that is, before the advent of civilisation. And so various 'state of nature' theories emerged in the writings of Hobbes, Locke, Rousseau and others. Some of these theories, however, were even more speculative than the 'natural law' theories they were attempting to replace; they differed sharply in their conclusions as to man's values and behaviour in the 'natural state'; and in any case they were more oriented to determining natural *rights* than natural law, and their conclusions (including various 'social contract' theories) thus became more relevant to political and legal philosophy than to ethics.

3(b) 1.32. Other empirically oriented thinkers, who wanted to remain on the level of ethics and avoid controversies about man's original 'natural state', were led, as we shall see in the immediately following section, to a philosophy of social utility, which began to function as a substitute for, rather than a continuation of, 'natural law' theory.

### 3(b) 2. Benthamite 'Social Utility' as a Strictly Objective Norm

A great multitude of people are continually talking of the Law of Nature; and then they go on giving you their [personal] sentiments about what is right and what is wrong; and these sentiments, you are to understand, are so many chapters, and sections of the Law of Nature. . . . [The 'Natural Law' consists] in so many contrivances for avoiding the obligation of appealing to any external standard, and for prevailing upon the readers to accept of the author's sentiment or opinion as a reason, and that a sufficient one, for itself.

Nature has placed mankind under the governance of two sovereign masters, *pain* and *pleasure*. . . . The *principle of utility* recognizes this subjection. . . . An action may be said to be conformable to the principle of utility . . . when the tendency it has to augment the happiness of the community is greater than any it has to diminish it.

Jeremy Bentham (1748–1832)[99]

The 'natural law' theories we have considered thrived in a mental environment which was characterised by a stable idea of nature; and also by belief in God, belief in some form of divine providence, and belief in some concept of eternal reward (or punishment) in an afterlife. During the eighteenth century Enlightenment, this mental environment was radically altered. Stoic and Aristotelian concepts of nature were considered passé, and were replaced with a more tentative, experimental approach; the providential God of Christianity and also of Stoicism was replaced with the God of deism, who winds up the clockwork mechanism of the world and lets it wind down along its inevitable course; the idea of a heaven and hell were dismissed as unhealthy, escapist, religious superstitions, and were replaced by secular, 'this-worldly' ideals.

The philosophy of social utility, which is now usually referred to as 'utilitarianism', became the perfect exemplar of the new attitudes fostered by the Enlightenment. It displaced the putative sovereignty of God with an acknowledgement of the 'real' sovereignty of the twin masters, pleasure and pain, over human behaviour. It replaced the idea of a Kingdom of God awaiting us in the next life, with the idea of a human and humane kingdom of happiness, attainable – at least for a majority – in this present life. It abandoned the ideal of modelling ourselves on nature, for a more active and scientific ideal: analysing the social mechanism, and working systematically, through proper planning and distribution, to maximise its total complement of pleasure and minimise the pains.

Here was a replacement for 'natural law' in a newly secularised, scientific, emancipated, democratised mankind. It was, as Bentham put it, an 'external standard' of morality for the individual as well as for leaders and administrators. And with the increased democratisation of political structures (which was another aspiration of the Enlightenment), the distinction between individuals and their leaders or administrators would have to become increasingly insignificant.

Jeremy Bentham's idea of utilitarianism, considered foundational in the development of modern Anglo-American ethical theory, had some important forerunners. The Frenchman Claude-Adrien Helvetius (1715–71) and the Scotsmen Francis Hutcheson (1694–1747) and David Hume (1711–76) gave quite clear expression to the 'principle of utility'. Bentham is especially indebted to Hutcheson (although, as Garry Wills shows,[100] the influence of Hutcheson on Bentham seems to have been largely indirect, through the writings of Cesare Beccaria). Hutcheson had not only coined the famous 'formula' of utilitarianism, '. . . the greatest happiness of the greatest number', but had even tried to develop elaborate algebraic formulas for calculating the individual's virtue of benevolence (that is, dedication to the production of the greatest happiness for the greatest number).[101] Bentham differs from Hutcheson, however, in two important respects: (a) he was not so much interested in the development of the subjective virtue of benevolence as in the presentation of a truly objective norm for moral behaviour; and (b) he was more hedonistically egalitarian, in the sense that for him the pleasures of one person cannot count for more than those of another, nor is there any important distinction between 'higher' and 'lower' pleasures.

Bentham's utilitarianism differs markedly from 'natural law' theories, in so far as it replaces the reverence for an invisible, metaphysically apprehended 'nature' with a respect for the new, observable and experiencable 'sovereigns', pleasure and pain; and in so far as it is also more explicitly geared to democratic social structures, in which due regard for the desires of the majority is paramount. But his utilitarianism also functions as a timely replacement for the 'natural law' theories. Just as the latter provided (or claimed to provide) certain objective norms for judging the behaviour of all men, without exception; so also utilitarianism, as expounded by Bentham, proposes a 'truly objective' (scientific) means of judging (calculating) the morality (usefulness) of all behaviour, without exception. When, for example, Bentham speaks of the measurement of 'units of pleasure', he is not speaking metaphorically, but giving expression to an optimism (rampant in the Enlightenment) about being able to measure precisely even human and social values. Bentham did not go to the Hutchesonian extreme of presenting algebraic formulas for measuring units of pleasure, but he did maintain that it is possible to compare pleasures in quantitative intensity and in respect to the number of individuals who would participate in them, and even prepared rather elaborate tables enumerating the various species of pleasure and pain.

When someone, especially one sympathetic to the liberal democratic Western tradition, first encounters the Benthamite theory of utility, he is struck at first by a certain elegant simplicity which seems to characterise it. Offhand it seems to cut through all the incessant subjective disputes about what is right and wrong and present us with a formula which, when used thoughtfully after investigation of the facts, will present us with clear-cut ethical norms. But as we begin reflecting on its implications and applications, all sorts of problems begin to rear their ugly heads: is happiness to be identified with pleasure, as Bentham thought? If so, are there 'higher' and 'lower' pleasures? Isn't it possible that doing one's duty, in Kantian fashion, could bring happiness? What if 'the greatest number of people' were Kantians, to whom doing duty was more important than pleasure? How would one maximise *their* happiness? Is the 'principle of utility' an 'ought' or an 'is' (in other words, is the maximisation of pleasure something we 'should' be oriented to, or a psychological *fact*, as Bentham thought?)? Even if we agree that all persons seek to maximise their own happiness or pleasure (egoism), how do we come to the conclusion that all seek or should seek to maximise the happiness of the majority (which seems to imply altruism)? In making utilitarian calculations, should we concentrate on the sum total of happiness resulting from the *act* (as Bentham supposed), or on the general consequences for happiness of this *type* of act (that is, this *rule*)? If (as seems likely) we have to choose between producing maximum happiness for a minority or minimal happiness for a majority, what does the utilitarian principle instruct us to do (the principle seems to be at least ambiguous, and possibly even self-contradictory on this point)? When I visualise some future state of happiness which I am planning to produce, how can I be sure that those whom I wish to benefit will have the proper physical and mental dispositions to benefit from what I finally end up doing? If those whom I wish to benefit appear to have a mistaken notion of what will make them happy, can I do something beneficial that they *think* will make them unhappy? If I contribute to the general welfare because I am genuinely concerned about others, am I not morally better than someone who does so for some less noble reason, for example, just to gain sufficient popularity to be elected to public office? (In other words, doesn't the *intention* make a difference?) If the majority believe that their happiness depends on the subjugation or extermination of a minority, can I help in the subjugation or extermination of that minority? If I have a choice of saving only one of two people from a burning building, one of whom is a scientist whose discoveries will make innumerable people happy, and the other of whom is the maid, who happens to be my mother, and who makes only me happy – must I save the scientist? If I make a contract and later discover that it will cause unhappiness to the majority of people who will be affected, must I break the contract?

The preceding paragraph offers just a sampling of actual questions that have been posed in the critical analysis of utilitarianism during the last two centuries. In response to such questions, great minds such as J. S. Mill, Henry Sidgwick, G. E. Moore and Bertrand Russell have taken up the challenge and developed more refined versions of utilitarianism, designed to satisfy the critics. The process of refining and revising utilitarianism has produced multiple branches and sub-branches: hedonistic *vs* ideal utilitarianism; descriptive *vs* normative; egotistical *vs* universalistic; restricted *vs* extreme; act-utilitarianism *vs* rule utilitarianism; primitive-rule-utilitarianism *vs* actual-rule-utilitarianism *vs* ideal-rule-utilitarianism; and so on. In short, controversy about utilitarianism is rife even among utilitarians themselves. *Why, then, does interest in and dedication to utilitarianism remain constantly high, especially among English-speaking ethicists?* The following reasons may be adduced:

3(b) 2.1.   There is a sense in which the pursuit of pleasure is a psychological fact, if not a 'law of nature', which can be ignored only at our peril if we want to make viable and relevant moral decisions. We need not agree with Bentham (and after him Sigmund Freud, B. F. Skinner and others) that the 'pleasure principle' is a primary fact of life in order to recognise that hedonistic considerations should have some place in our ethical thinking.

3(b)   2.2.  Utilitarianism is eminently compatible with individualistic liberal democratic structures which are oriented *politically* to procuring 'the greatest happiness for the greatest number'. If they fail to do this they must end up in anarchy, on the one hand, or in dictatorship, on the other. In such societies, practical utilitarianism is a necessity, and utilitarian theory may be an appropriate complement to utilitarian praxis.

3(b) 2.3.   For those who cannot accept a traditional 'natural law' theory, utilitarianism, at least in the original Benthamite version, offers an alternative means of discerning and delineating objective moral norms for behaviour. Even atheists and empiricists, who are impatient of 'divine' or *'a priori'* moral norms, may be unwilling to offer the palm of victory to the subjectivists,[102] the relativists,[103] or the emotivists.[104] But those utilitarians who, in their zeal for accommodating actual or possible objections to Bentham's principles, develop more sophisticated versions of utilitarianism (rule utilitarianism, ideal utilitarianism, etc.), bringing in qualifications or modifications which exemplify subjective ingenuity but not a neat and solid objectivity, risk departing from the objectivity which had been one of the most important claims to credibility in Bentham's theory.

3(b) 2.4.   An alternative to *revising and modifying* Bentham's theory, and thus diminishing its objectivity, would be to *limit its scope* to those cases in which human decision-making is concerned with acts which (a) have an effect on the basic pleasures or satisfactions of others; (b) involve choices between clear-cut alternatives, one of which will appreciably maximise the happiness of the other persons involved, more than the other alternatives; (c) involve choices on the part of those who have some responsibility for the happiness of others; and (d) especially involve choices on the part of those who have some official or publicly recognised responsibility for the happiness of others – for example, legislators and those who, like Bentham himself did, are lobbying or working in some way for social reform. The latter sorts of activities will often involve certain decisions which could have a clear and appreciable effect on the basic welfare or quality of life of many. In Bentham's time, it was his 'utilitarian' thinking that led him to work for universal adult male literacy, secret ballots, annual Parliamentary sessions, free trade, public sanitation, prison reform, reformulation of the laws in terms intelligible to laymen, and other progressive liberal causes; in many of these campaigns, he was ultimately successful.

3(b) 2.5.   Utilitarianism, at least in its Benthamite form, is a solidly objective moral theory. It goes beyond the aesthetic/moral realm, which is concerned to a great extent with conformity to existing social norms, sometimes promulgated and enforced by the few in power, and asks us to search out ways of acting which will be beneficial to larger and larger contingents of people. The 'expanding circle' syndrome, discussed at the beginning of this chapter,[105] is clearly bolstered by the application of utilitarian principles. Judiciously applied, utilitarian principles would eventually extend not just to the majority in our society, but to the majority of people in the world, and perhaps even to future generations. But if we are looking for a theory which clearly applies right now to world majorities, or *all* human beings or future generations, we will not find such universality and breadth explicitly in utilitarianism.

## 3(b) 3.   Marxism

Just as Darwin discovered the law of development of organic nature, so Marx discovered the law of development of human history. . . . Marx also discovered the special law of motion governing the present-day capitalist mode of production and the bourgeois society that this mode of production has created.
Friedrich Engels, graveside eulogy for Karl Marx[106]

He who would criticize all human acts, movements, relations, etc. by the principle of utility [utilitarianism], must first deal with human nature in general, and then with human nature as modified in each historical epoch. Bentham makes short work of it. With the driest naïveté he takes the modern shopkeeper, especially the English shopkeeper, as the normal man. Whatever is useful to this queer normal man, and to his world, is absolutely useful.

[Dialectics] regards every historically developed form as being in a fluid state, in motion, and therefore grasps its transient aspect as well. . . . The fact that the movement of capitalist society is full of contradictions impresses itself most strikingly on the practical bourgeois in the changes of the periodic cycle through which modern industry passes, the summit of which is the 'general crisis'. . . . The intensity of [the impact of a general crisis] will drum dialectics even into the heads of the upstarts in charge.

Karl Marx (1818–83)[107]

The workingmen have no country. . . . National differences and antagonisms between peoples are daily vanishing, owing to . . . uniformity in the mode of production and in the conditions of life corresponding thereto. . . . The supremacy of the proletariat will cause [these differences] to vanish still faster. . . . In proportion as the exploitation of one individual by another is put to an end, the exploitation of one nation by another will also be put to an end.

Marx and Engels[108]

Karl Marx in some places denies that his 'dialectical' system – called 'dialectical materialism' by Engels but described by others as 'historical materialism' – was a system of 'morality'.[109] But Marx's denial has to be understood in the same way that a Stoic would have had to be understood when he advocated going beyond the conventional, provincial moral codes of his time. In other words, Marx, like the Stoics, was advocating going beyond a certain confining, restricted set of moral norms – in his case, 'bourgeois' morality. The ongoing dispute about whether Marxism expounds a system of morality is mainly a dispute about terminology. If we accept 'morality' in the broad sense, as a system having to do with right and wrong in human behaviour, Marx is certainly concerned with morality.[110] In terms of the categories we have been using in our analysis, Marxism is a system which propounds objective norms derived both from nature and from mankind. And one could say that Marxism's claim on the attention of ethicists derives from its attempt to avoid and transcend two deficiencies in Benthamite utilitarianism: (a) the fact that Bentham's utilitarianism is based on the presumption of a natural drive (for the pursuit of pleasure), *without* relating this presumption to any clear concept of nature; and (b) the fact that the philosophy of social utility is concerned with maximising a narrow, bourgeoise version of 'pleasure' within the context of the *essentially* exploitive capitalistic systems of the eighteenth and nineteenth centuries. In contrast, Marxism (a) is based on a quasi-scientific concept (some Marxists would drop the 'quasi-', and some critics of Marxism would substitute 'pseudo-' for 'quasi-') of a dialectical progression of nature, applied by Marx himself primarily to socio-economic evolution, and by Engels even more broadly to the sub-human strata of nature; and (b) goes beyond the 'bourgeois democratic' aims of utilitarian majoritarianism, to embrace the cause of the welfare of all men in a nonexploitive, classless, explicitly international society.

### 3(b) 3.1.  *Marxism as a Conception of Evolving Nature*

In 1860 Marx read Charles Darwin's *On the Origin of Species*, which had just recently been published. He was very sympathetic to Darwin's theory of evolution, and wrote to Engels (19 December 1860) that 'this is the book that contains the biological basis of our conceptions'. In 1873, Marx sent a complimentary copy of the new edition of his *Das Kapital* to Darwin, and Darwin, within a few weeks, acknowledged receipt of the book, adding that both Marx and himself 'earnestly desire the extension of knowledge'.[111] Some claim that Marx proposed to dedicate the English translation of the second volume of *Das Kapital* to Darwin, but recently discovered evidence has rendered this contention doubtful. In any case, there is little doubt that Marx was immensely impressed by Darwin and his scientific methodology.[112]

Marx became disenchanted with various capitalist and socialist misapplications of the biological concepts of 'survival of the fittest' and 'struggle for existence', and disagreed with Darwin's espousal of the Malthusian theory of population. And so Engels's graveside comparison could be misconstrued. However, Marx's diffidence about aspects of Darwinism did not prevent him from subscribing to the principle of an evolving nature. And indeed Marx's theory, which is concerned with the development of socio-economic relations from primitive times through feudalism and capitalism to communism, is an extension in a general way of the principle of evolution to social relations. There are ongoing controversies as to whether and how Marx effected an amalgamation of philosophically inspired 'dialectic' with the methods of empirical science, which Marx had to use to develop a 'scientific' socialism. What seems clear and incontrovertible, however, is that Marx theorised, and was conscious of theorising, about the history of socio-economic relations somewhat after the manner that Darwin theorised about the natural history of the biological species – tracing the 'natural' progression from lower to higher forms.

In 'natural law' theories, as we saw, a prime imperative was man's conformity to 'nature' conceived as a system of regular cycles or a fixed hierarchical system. When nature, especially human nature, is construed as necessarily involved in a dialectical-evolutionary *process*, a new kind of 'natural law' is called for: 'understand the natural dialectical process taking place in history, live in conformity with it, and work to foster it and even accelerate it'. Behind this reasoning there is, of course, the unprovable presupposition that the evolutionary processes are progressive, are leading to something better. Through scientifically analysable 'tendencies' (rather that metaphysical 'teleology'), a final stage would be achieved, a communistic society in which man's natural and primary 'need for other men' would be realised. For Marx, 'morality' consisted in a person's conscious alignment of himself with evolving human nature and with its progression to a higher, more socialised level, a progression that was taking place in an evolutionary manner, but could be facilitated in a revolutionary manner involving man's conscious intervention and co-operation.

*3(b) 3.2.   Marxism as a Theory of Universal Fulfilment and Solidarity*
We have discussed already[113] some of the developments in the eighteenth-century Enlightenment which utilitarianism capitalised upon and assimilated. Marxism goes even further than utilitarianism in bringing these developments to a logical conclusion:

3(b) 3.21.   *From secularism to atheism:* Marxism not only seeks to develop an ethical theory independent of religious overtones (the belief in God, the creation of nature, and divine providence), but seeks to abolish religion entirely. Marx's final incentive for doing this came largely from his study of the theory of Ludwig Feuerbach who, in his *The Essence of Christianity* (1841) argued that the belief in God was not only not necessary for, but a positive obstacle to, the moral development of mankind. Feuerbach's reasoning was based on a concept of a mechanism somewhat similar to what contemporary psychoanalysts call 'projection', except that psychoanalysts usually use the term in a negative sense, for example, to describe the way that a person may try to get rid of guilt feelings by 'projecting' the guilt on to someone else. In Feuerbach's theory the 'projection mechanism' – if I may use that term – is concerned with positive qualities that we project on to some imagined divine being. For example, we have within ourselves unlimited powers of love, which could be channelled in effective concern for other men. Instead, by developing the concept of an 'all-loving' God who will 'provide' for others while we pursue our own interests and aggrandisement, we escape from the necessity of dealing with, and activating, these latent powers. According to Feuerbach, man's immense latent powers for knowledge and power, as well as love, remain inactive because so many men are content to abide with the fictional ideal of a God who is supposed to activate these powers. Feuerbach, however, did not draw any radical political conclusions from his critique. Marx, the revolutionary, did not hesitate to draw such conclusions: we must abolish religion, the 'opium of the people', and the false hope of salvation which it offers, if we are ever to activate in the masses a consciousness of the social progress of which they are capable.

3(b) 3.22.   *From majoritarianism to universalism:* Utilitarianism in its basic *concept* did not make any discriminatory distinctions between persons. One person's pleasure was just as important as another's. And, as we saw, there were no specific ethnic, racial or national boundaries explicitly drawn as to *whose* happiness we should primarily seek. The inculcation by utilitarianism of a commitment to 'the greatest happiness of the greatest number' represented a great advance in social consciousness over the more élitist eras of the past, whose denizens would never have even thought it possible that any substantial material happiness could be obtained by any more than a minority of mankind. And theoretically, the 'principle of utility' *could* apply to 'the greatest happiness of the greatest number of

people' in the *world*. But *practically* speaking, utilitarianism
flourished in industrialised capitalist countries, in which a relatively
well-situated middle class or 'bourgeoisie', whether or not it
constituted an absolute majority, knew that 'the greatest happiness
of the greatest number' was a prerequisite, if revolution, civil strife,
and destruction of parliamentary institutions were to be avoided.
Conscientious utilitarians such as Bentham were willing to provide
for the welfare of the lowest strata of society, the 'proletariat'
included. But this provision was to depend on personal initiative or
generosity, as well as on the intermittent benevolence of legislators,
administrators and judges. Capitalism's need of an ever-ready
labour force would dictate such benevolence, but there was no
explicit provision in utilitarian principles for an overthrow of the
oppressive class system which made the proletariat inescapably
dependent on the benevolence of the bourgeoisie, even if, through
cyclical economic crises, the proletariat became the majority.
Marxism, on the other hand, does not just envision the economic
and social betterment of the proletariat, but inverts the whole class
system, putting the proletariat, 'the universal class',[114] on top. The
idea was that, if the proletariat (that is, primarily ordinary working
men and women) were given preference and put in charge,
self-perpetuating class divisions and antagonisms would fall by the
wayside. And capitalism itself, by organising the proletariat into an
ever larger and more unified working force, would inadvertently
bring about the social organisation necessary for the takeover of the
territory and prerogatives of the masters (landowners, industrialists
and their political and ideological confederates) by the slaves (the
proletariat) on whom they had become too dependent. The result,
after an interim 'dictatorship of the proletariat', would be a
universal, international communist society, in which the forces of
production and the powers of distribution would actually be in the
hands of those who do the producing: the workers themselves.

3(b) 3.23.   *From needs to need:* Utilitarianism was concerned with the
fulfilment of human needs. In Bentham's theory, there was no
significant theoretical discrimination between natural and acquired,
unconditional and conditioned, higher and lower needs, although
there was a practical commitment to the fulfilment of basic needs for
the underprivileged through social welfare programmes and
legislation. Marx, on the other hand, criticises the creation by
antisocial economic structures of certain artificially conditioned

needs (for example, for prostitution, drugs, alcohol, conspicuous luxury), and points out that there is one primary or 'higher' need that is hardly being fulfilled at all under modern forms of economic-social organisation – namely, the need for other people.[115] It is in terms of this insight that one can understand Marx's critical attitude towards social reformers like Bentham. In Marx's estimation, such men were concentrating too much on the deleterious *effects* of defective social relations, while largely leaving the causes intact. Marx's prescription: alter the socio-economic structures in such a way as (a) to reflect the basic need of human beings *for one another*, and (b) to guarantee the fulfilment of this need, by doing away with socio-economic relations which foster and perpetuate social alienation. The fulfilment of the other various needs, including especially the needs for the various necessities of life, will follow from the very nature of the new socialised society, and of the newly socialised human beings who would make up this society.

Flaws in Marxism are now rather widely known and acknowledged, at least in the 'Western' bloc: Marx's prediction of a 'necessary' progression to communism through capitalism has never taken place; the labour forces have often participated in the progress of capitalism, or at least the working men have not consistently developed a consciousness of themselves as an alienated revolutionary 'proletariat'; many of the predictions of Marx about the limits of growth and about progressive impoverishment under capitalism have apparently not come true; his theory of value is not taken seriously even by most Marxist economists; his vision of a 'classless' society that would result under communism has certainly not come true in any Marxist regime; the predicted international *esprit de corps* among communists from various countries has not materialised.

In spite of such flaws, which are recognised by some in the Soviet bloc and the 'third world' as well as in capitalist countries, the attraction of Marxism persists and even grows. Why is this? The two aspects of 'objectivity' that we touched on above may have something to do with the apparent *moral* appeal of Marxism: (a) Marxism as an *evolutionary* socioethical theory offers a modern, post-Enlightenment means for grounding morality in 'nature' (dialectically interpreted), thus filling the vacuum left by the weakness of ostensibly outdated and static 'natural law' theories[116] and the lack of a solid scientific or metaphysical concept of nature in utilitarianism; and (b) Marxism is the only major modern ethical system which holds forth, like Stoicism in the Roman world, the vision of an international community, universal equality, and the abolition of oppression – objective ideals just as attractive in the modern era, as in the days of Stoicism. Or, to put the matter in a slightly different way, if someone were searching for a strictly secular moral theory which combined a modern evolutionary concept of human nature with an ideal of universal brotherhood, where but to Marxism could he or she go?

Like Stoicism, Marxism has just a few identifiable moral imperatives associated with it: non-exploitation, equality, dedication to justice ('from each according to his ability, to each according to his needs') and communitarianism. The basic defects of contemporary Marxist–Leninist theory – its widely disputed dialectical interpretation of nature and history, and its emphasis on social unity at the expense of individual rights and freedoms – have apparently not been serious enough to counteract the appeal of the above moral imperatives.

Would it not be possible to develop a formidable alternative to Marxism in an ethical system which would combine both (a) a scientifically respectable post-Darwinian view of social evolution, and (b) a credible, non-utopian vision of international harmony? In recent decades the widespread criticism which met biologist Julian Huxley's attempt to do just this has helped dissuade most philosophers from contemplating any such synthesis. Possibly the most successful synthesis of this sort is to be found in the evolutionary theory of Teilhard de Chardin which, because its thrust is primarily religious, will be considered in the next chapter.

### 3(c)  SOME ATTEMPTS AT ETHICAL CORRELATIVISM

It should be kept in mind that the differentiation we have made above between subjectively- and objectively-oriented theories is a matter of emphasis, not of exclusive concentration: the categorical imperative of Kant or the 'impartial spectator' theory of Smith are concerned primarily with subjective prerequisites, but do not exclude attention to objective norms, derived from nature or mankind; the Thomistic 'natural law' theory is primarily a statement about objective norms, but does not exclude consideration of subjective intentions; utilitarianism and Marxism also purport to provide objective norms, but do not ignore the value of subjective dispositions (in the one case, dedication to public welfare; in the other, commitment to revolutionary praxis).

Would it be possible to develop an ethical theory which explicitly and simultaneously emphasises both the subjective and the objective aspects or rather, emphasises the *correlation* between the two aspects? Several theories seem to be of this nature. Possibly because of their greater complexity, none of them is conspicuous at present as a leading moral theory – at least in their correlative form; but they are of interest in so far as they indicate an important direction for ethical theorising.

### 3(c) 1.  Hegel (1770–1831): the Good and Conscience

G. W. F. Hegel, a German philosopher whose social philosophy and ethics have been widely misinterpreted (by Marx, Kierkegaard and even some Hegelians) as an objectively oriented idealistic system, prefaces his discussion of social philosophy in *The Philosophy of Right* with a section on 'Morality' which expounds a correlativistic theory. According to Hegel, 'moral good' is synonymous with an objective equilibrium *in society* between 'the universal' (duty) and 'the particular' (individual rights); a dialectic is set up between *this objective equilibrium* and subjective *'conscience'*, whose task it is to bring about in the individual a personal equilibrium between rights and duty. The continual dialectic between conscience and a good society – both of which are continually testing and sometimes revising the relationship between rights and duties – is called 'ethical life' by Hegel (or, in the terminology we have used in this book, complete moral good).[117]

### 3(c) 2.  Nietzsche (1844–1900): the Will to Power and the Superman

Friedrich Nietzsche's existential philosophy could be characterised as a reaction against Darwinism, especially if we take into account some of the scattered notes he was making towards the end of his writing career, which were published posthumously under the title, *The Will to Power*.[118] Nietzsche, who in his *Genealogy of Morals* opposes the tendencies towards a 'herd mentality' in history and in modern society, looks with disdain on Darwin's doctrine of the 'survival of the fittest', according to which mere adaptibility and reproductive fecundity have often enabled masses of inferior organisms to survive at the expense of the higher (that is, more complex but less hardy) organisms. In place of Darwinian 'natural selection', Nietzsche hypothesises a 'will to power' existing even in inorganic matter, and causing the evolution of more and more powerful beings. The culmination of this hypothesised objective process is the 'superman', (*Übermensch*), an individual whose controlled and sublimated power is the source of creativity and a morally creative life. *Subjectively* speaking, the superman is the unique individual whose dedication to the evolution of the will to power in the world is so complete, spontaneous and unregretting that he can will an 'eternal recurrence' of the same processes and of the very way that he has participated in these processes, without a trace of resentment or the slightest wish that things 'could have been otherwise'.[119] By proving his mettle in this test, the superior individual 'selects himself out' (to use the Darwinian phrase); but it is also a function of *objectively* evolving life to 'select out' such individuals, to produce possibly a few supermen (even one, or the effort to produce one, would be enough) in this non-Darwinian way.[120]

### 3(c) 3. Dewey (1859–1952): Natural, Social and Personal Evolution

The American philosopher John Dewey was a philosophical pragmatist, and shared with other pragmatists the general objective of doing away with fixed and static ideas and principles, to which one adheres simply because of tradition, custom or faulty *a priori* reasoning. He describes his empirically oriented, pragmatic ethics as being based on an 'interaction between elements of human nature', on the one hand, and 'the environment, natural and social', on the other.[121] The 'natural environment' is portrayed by Dewey with moderately Darwinian overtones: it is an arena in which the processes of adaptation, interaction and change in the present continue the evolutionary processes of the past.[122] The 'social environment' is likewise a fluid dynamism of interaction, interdependency and change.[123] On the subjective side, the 'moral life' of the individual consists in the growth which results from his constant interaction and struggle with the challenges offered by his natural and social environment.[124] Thus the main moral imperative to be found in Dewey is the imperative of growth, or more precisely the personal imperative to understand, respond to, control and perhaps even surpass the processes of natural and social evolution in which one is involved because of his very existence.

The correlativism of these latter three theories is summarised in the following chart:

| | *Subjective intention* | *Objective norms* | *The characterisation of the moral good which results* |
|---|---|---|---|
| *Hegel* | Maintaining personal equilibrium of duties and rights in one's society | The constant equilibrium of duty and individual rights in (a free) society | 'Ethical life' |
| *Nietzsche* | Approximation to the ideal of the superman, through passing the test of 'eternal recurrence' | The Will to Power, which 'selects out' superior individuals, especially through devising the myth of 'eternal recurrence' | The collaboration of all elements of life to produce if possible a superman |
| *Dewey* | Constant pursuit of growth produced by interaction, adaptation and struggle with one's natural and social environment | Evolution itself, conceived as a process of struggle and growth, continuing and intensified in social evolution | Moral growth through pragmatic situational interaction of individuals and their environment |

## 3(d)  CONTEMPORARY TRENDS

It would be beyond the scope of our analysis to go into detail concerning contemporary ethical theories. But before proceeding further we may at least briefly show how many contemporary theories seem to exemplify, if not an 'eternal recurrence', at least a continuing resurgence, of some of the classical positions we have considered.

'Good reasons' theorists – such as P. H. Nowell Smith, Kurt Baier, and Stephen Toulmin – exemplify the very important and perhaps predominant thrust of ethics towards verification of rationality as the species-specific human subjective disposition (see above, section 3(a) 2). The 'good reason' ethicists hold that ethical judgements involve a unique reasoning process, unlike that, for example, in science. For moral behaviour it is necessary and

sufficient to give some practical justification (a good reason, based
on relevant facts) for one's choice of actions – a justification which
need not fit in with the precise patterns of inductive or deductive
logic.

Thomas Nagel, who speaks of 'putting yourself in the other
person's shoes' as the 'general form of moral reasoning'[125] is using
language obviously comparable to that of the Golden Rule (see
above, section 3(a) 2.1).

A number of contemporary positions are reminiscent of Adam
Smith's 'Impartial Spectator' theory (see above, section 3(a) 2.4).
Bruce Ackerman's 'neutral dialogue' among omniscient
participants,[126] and Dworkin's 'equal concern and respect'[127] seem
to function as subjective procedures for assuring impartiality as
does Adam Smith's theory. Peter Singer's 'perfectly sympathetic
spectator' is an explicit attempt to reformulate Adam Smith's
'impartial spectator' in a manner conducive to a utilitarian
approach.[128]

R. M. Hare and Marcus Singer, who maintain that prescriptive
ethical statements are of their very nature universal, are echoing the
first formulation of Kant's categorical imperative (see above, section
3(a) 2.5).[129] But what Hare and Singer call 'universalisation' – that is,
being willing to make the same ethical judgements in every
relevantly similar situation – is, strictly speaking, more akin to the
aspect of 'self-consistency' (see above, pp. 47, 54–5) than to the
aspect of 'universality' (see above, pp. 48, 54–5) in rational ethical
procedures. John Rawls's device of 'the veil of ignorance' – a means
of testing our attitude towards social justice by imagining ourself in
an 'original position' before any social system was constructed and
before we knew anything about our own social and economic status
– is somewhat similar to Kant's third formulation of the categorical
imperative (see above, section 3(a) 4), except that Rawls adds
contemporary liberal democratic 'riders' concerning liberty and
provision for the 'worst off'.[130]

Most reminiscent of the cosmopolitan, ecumenical spirit of the
Stoics (see above, section 3(b) 1.1) are the contemporary 'world
order theorists', who co-ordinate the insights of many disciplines to
develop workable and credible models of a peaceful world order to
replace the nationalistically-oriented 'balance of power' model
which currently dominates political theorising internationally and
threatens to self-destruct.[131] Among more traditional philosophers,
Josiah Royce also advocated an ecumenical ideal – a great world

community in which all major antagonisms would be transcended in the interests of a common humanity.[132]

As was indicated above (section 3(b) 1.3), 'natural law' theory, at least outside the Catholic tradition, has tended to become more and more empirical since the time of Grotius. A recent description of a 'naturalistic' position by D. D. Raphael, for example, seems to be a continuation of lines of thought established by Grotius:

> All societies think that it is wrong to hurt members of their own group at least (or to kill them unless there are morally compelling reasons); that it is right to keep faith; that the needy should be helped; that people who deliberately flout the accepted rules should be punished.[133]

David Little has even gone further than these common-sense observations, arguing for a natural law grounded in empirical generalisation drawn from the work of cultural anthropologists.[134]

A simple deference to the prevalence of various value-orientations in a *single* society would be what we characterised in Chapter 2 as recognition of objective aesthetic/moral norms. If we were to go further, as Raphael and Little seem to do, and conclude, 'since such-and-such value-orientations are found in *all* societies, they may give evidence of a natural law' – we would be deriving, in Grotian fashion, the natural law from the *jus gentium*.

It would be inaccurate to speak of a contemporary 'resurgence' or 'reflection' of Thomistic natural law (see section 3(b) 1.2), of utilitarianism (section 3(b) 2), or of Marxism (section 3(b) 3), since all three theories are still in full vigour in the Western world, constituting 'schools' of moral philosophy. A relationship of Thomistic natural law theory to Catholicism will be discussed in the following section. The proliferation of branches and sub-branches of utilitarianism is so extensive that it would be misleading for me to pinpoint any individual philosopher or school as carrying on the 'themes' of utilitarianism. A similar observation can be made about Marxism, in which the branching-out process, if we add Soviet, East European, Latin-American and Chinese interpretations to the Western, has been even more prolific than in utilitarianism.

### 3(e)   THE MORAL/RELIGIOUS SPHERE

Before turning our attention in the next chapter to the religious sphere, we should take notice of an intermediate area, in which there is a sometimes ambiguous amalgam between moral theory and religion.

Two of the best-known amalgams are to be found in the Roman Catholic church. This world-wide religious organisation is officially committed to Thomistic 'natural law' theory, which is often referred to in pronouncements on moral/religious matters. For instance, the claim that 'according to the natural law' sexual intercourse is necessarily related to reproduction was foundational in Pope Paul VI's encyclical *Humanae vitae* on birth control. [135] On an unofficial but increasingly important level, Marxism, or at least the Marxist concept of revolutionary praxis in overcoming socio-economic exploitation has influenced Catholic 'liberation theology', whose primary appeal has been in South and Central America. On the more subjective side, the influence of existentialist ethics on both Catholic and Protestant theology, in the work of Karl Rahner, Rudolph Bultmann and Karl Barth, and of existential phenomenology on the ethical writings of Pope John Paul II, constitute some of the more overt twentieth-century ethical-religious amalgams. And finally, utilitarianism, which is an implicit assumption in liberal democratic societies, has undoubtedly had at least a latent influence on writings and policies in liberal Christian social thought, Catholic as well as Protestant.

It is interesting to note that in moral theology (or Christian ethics) Protestants generally favour the more subjective ethical theories, such as existentialism, while Catholics tend towards the more objective theories, such as natural law ethics. James Gustafson sees these tendencies as natural results of the traditional Protestant emphasis on subjective dispositions and intentions, and the traditional Catholic emphasis on conformity to objective laws and norms. [136] He notes that a gradual *rapprochement* is developing as both Protestants and Catholics strive to overcome the one-sidedness of their respective theories. One might surmise that an attempt at correlativism is proceeding at a faster pace on the moral/religious level than at the strictly moral level.

# 4

# Religious Good and the Common Good

## ARGUMENT

*Religion, at least as practised and expounded by the world's major religions, is not concerned solely or even primarily with inculcating moral dispositions or behaviour, but aspires, if such a thing is possible, to go beyond mere morality. In this chapter we consider the religious motivations which lead to such an aspiration, and also lead to positive and concrete guidelines for establishing and consolidating a supra-moral sphere of human living. Having differentiated a specifically religious good from moral and aesthetic good, we will turn briefly, for the sake of comprehensivity, to differentiate another somewhat divergent concept, 'the common good', which in common usage also seems to be further subdivided into economic, political and legal applications and implications.*

Sometimes the word 'good' is ascribed to individuals or groups in a way that is neither precisely aesthetic nor precisely moral. For example, certain religious acts or characteristics may be called 'good'; and the extremely common idea of the 'common good', which all individuals and groups should presumably promote, is used with a number of connotations which shade off into one another, inviting some differentiation and comment. Before attempting in the next chapter to give a final definition and differentiation of the morally good, we should examine religious good and the common good, which involve concepts and usages somewhat similar to, but also somewhat different from, both the aesthetic and the moral usage and concept.

## 4(a)  RELIGIOUS GOOD

A clarification of the notion of religious good may perhaps best be
approached by a consideration of certain limitations, drawbacks or
deficiencies which are largely unavoidable in the *moral* sphere.

The cultivation of the proper subjective disposition, intention or
attitude is, as we saw in the last chapter, indispensible to moral
behaviour. But the process of cultivating these aspects is
characterised as an internal conflict and struggle – more markedly in
the theories of, say, Kant, Sartre, or Kierkegaard, but also in the
theories of Aristotle and Spinoza. The moral person, we may well
conclude, is an alienated person, one who is at odds with himself,
caught between duty and inclination, freedom and compromise, the
ideal self and the real self, reason and passion, virtue and weakness
(or 'incontinence', as the Aristotelian term is sometimes translated).
There is, indeed, an unavoidable negative element in the moral
point of view. A certain amount of Socratic dissatisfaction with self –
intolerance of one's own smugness or conceit – is of the essence.
Carried to an extreme, this dissatisfaction can result in guilt and
despair, be an impediment to any moral activity, issue in neuroses
and psychoses, even in violent crime. But at a more *moderate* level it
supplies that healthy psychic tension without which there can be no
dynamic moral development. Kierkegaard says, as we saw in the
last chapter, that there is only one moral choice – the choice of self.
We might go further and say that the choice of self is a choice of
alienation, a choice of constant disparity with, and pursuit of, one's
ideal self. One may want to approximate the ideal, but actually to
attain it (or think one has attained it) once and for all would stop all
further psychological movement, would arrest further
development. Therefore the maintenance of a modest tension
between one's ideal self and real self – to continue with the
Kierkegaardian terminology – is itself a second-order ideal. To be
committed to this second-order ideal is to be committed to the
perpetuation of a subjective state of at least moderate alienation.

Theories which are concerned with *objective* norms encounter a
more external species of alienation. Natural law theorists find
themselves committed to 'laws of nature' – for example, with regard
to birth control – which a significantly large group of human beings
do not find it 'natural' to obey; utilitarians find their optimism about
producing 'the greatest happiness for the greatest number'
dampened by the fact that most individuals seem narcissistically

committed only to their own happiness and possibly that of a coterie with which they identify; Marxists must be disillusioned by the fact that the proletariat of the world, which was in Marx's calculations supposed to be the spearhead of the communist revolution, seems to lack commitment, and to require constant prodding from the more committed intellectuals, ideologues, demogogues or bureaucrats.

Even the 'correlativists', who have elaborated some extraordinarily harmonious and integrated relationships on the purely theoretical level, find in practical reality a source of alienation. Hegel's dialectical reciprocity of rights and duties was not reflected in the Prussia in which he lived, and to this day is not to be found in any actually existing state; Nietzsche's most promising candidates for designation as 'supermen' turn out on Nietzsche's own closer scrutiny to be 'all too human'; Dewey's exhortation to growth by meeting situational and environmental challenges founders when, as most often happens, individuals prefer comfort to challenge, or find the challenges are overwhelming and disheartening.

Thus the moral theorist, and his practical counterpart, the moralist, take on an ironic, quixotic aspect, aptly characterised in Hegel's somewhat satirical phenomenology of the 'Knight of Virtue'.[1] Even Thomists, utilitarians and Marxists, none of whom consider themselves philosophical idealists, turn out to be idealists in the wide sense – over-enamoured of a theory which is belied in the sphere of practical experience. An ethical person or ethicist who proposes to avoid the various alienations associated with the moral point of view may desire in desperation to revert to the amoral or 'aesthetic' sphere – a reversion whose possibility is seriously to be doubted, if we are to believe Kierkegaard.[2]

But there is yet another means of avoiding both external and internal alienation – religion.

Religion? An escape from alienation? Has not religion had more than a moderate share of responsibility for exacerbating human self-alienation – sometimes to the extremes of psychosis and suicide? and social alienation – sometimes to the extremes of war and revolution? One might answer such allegations by saying in a facile manner that the allegations refer to 'religion', not (bona fide) religion; or (using Kierkegaard's terminology), to Christendom, not to Christianity. But however we wish to classify or explain such disintegrative phenomena, there is also an integrative or harmonising aspect of religion, in both the intrapsychic and the social spheres, which should not be ignored and may be of the utmost importance. Let me explain.

The thrust of religion, in its integrative/subjective aspects, is towards the attainment of a simple, harmonious, non-alienated experience of a consciousness which goes beyond the bounds of morality. In the Christian religion, this religious experience is variously referred to as 'being in the state of grace', 'union with God', 'having the (Holy) Spirit', 'being saved', 'being born again'. In Buddhism, *Satori* ('Enlightenment'); in Hinduism, Yoga ('Union') are parallel concepts. The religious experience allows of varying degrees of intensity, the highest degree of which is a state of constant or habitual union with God, sometimes called 'the unitive state' in Christian mysticism, *Nirvana* in Buddhism, *Samahdi* in Hinduism. In such a state, it is maintained, one is 'free from the law' (of duty and morality), and possesses an interior impetus or 'unction' which leads him or her quasi-instinctively to do what is right.[3] It is only in this state that one can, in the words of St Augustine, or of the twentieth-century theologian Dietrich Bonhoeffer, 'love God, and do what you like'. This state amounts to a final reversal of the 'original sin' described in *Genesis*, which consisted in forsaking the 'tree of life' (simple personal union with God) for the 'tree of knowledge of good and evil' (the attempt to work out *all* the details of right and wrong by human ingenuity or ratiocination).[4] In its less mystical intensities, this same religious spirit gives religious individuals the *inclination* to do their *duty* (thus overcoming the Kantian dichotomy), and gives them the ability or power to go *beyond* the requirements of duty to do works of supererogation or charity. One who is characterised by even the lesser degrees of this religious spirit can purportedly avoid the alienation caused by morality, by living habitually on a higher plane, in which calculations concerning multifarious duties or moral choices are rendered relatively unnecessary, or at least less difficult or less complex, by virtue of one's union with the supervening divine life-force or spirit. The means for arriving at such a state may, of course, involve both difficulty and complexity – possibly long periods of self-discipline, ascetic practices, meditation exercises, or even formal vows (as in monasticism) of poverty, chastity and/or obedience. But to the extent that the state is finally attained, morality is replaced by a single impulse, which cannot strictly be characterised as an 'ought', and is summed up in the simple commandment, 'love God and love your neighbour'.

Religion in its integrative/objective aspects is oriented towards overcoming bumbling secular class systems, institutions and organisations, and their endemic conflicts, by ultimately building up a harmonious, voluntary, international community, the objective counterpart to the voluntariness and spontaneity which are also found in individual religious experience. In Christianity, the form that this organisation takes is largely determined by the particular Christian denomination's interpretation of the 'Kingdom of God' spoken of in the Gospel. If the 'Kingdom of God' is relegated to the afterlife, the organisation in this life will be primarily a mobilisation to prepare for the next life. If the 'Kingdom' is thought of as beginning in this life, more or less concrete efforts will be made to build a visible, non-alienated universal community in this life. The highest degree of both visibility and ecumenicity has been claimed by the Catholic Church, which emphasises a world-wide doctrinal and ritual uniformity to maintain and foster the development of a non-alienated 'people of God', existing right alongside, or even in the midst of, the alienated social and political systems of the world. The 'ecumenical movement' in the Catholic Church is an attempt to extend this process beyond the boundaries of denominational Catholicism. A somewhat more diversified Protestant counterpart to Catholic ecumenism is the World Council of Churches.

The tendency to build up an international voluntary association of believers is also noticeable in other major world religions – in the worldwide networks of Buddhist meditation centres, in the Hindu inspired transmission of yoga techniques (and the contemporary secularised version, 'transcendental meditation') throughout the world, and in the spread of the Islamically inspired and explicitly ecumenical Baha'i religion.

If we consider the external relationships of the major religious establishments among themselves, we often find intense, long-lasting and bloody conflicts. Conflicts are also to be found, of course, among rival sects of the same religion. But if we look to the explicitly ecumenical networks emerging out of each of the major religions, we receive an impression more of harmony than of conflict, and can perceive the possibility that these ecumenical efforts may even eventually merge, and serve to counterbalance secular disunion, as the British historian, Arnold Toynbee, has optimistically suggested.[5] In this event, the integrative power of religion could effectively rival the power of even the most ecumenical ethical systems for defusing social alienation.

A final religious vision which involves a reinterpretation not only of society but also of nature, and is 'correlativistic' in the sense adumbrated in Chapter 3, is the scientific–philosophical–theological synthesis of the French Jesuit paleontologist, Pierre Teilhard de Chardin (1881–1955).[6] Teilhard takes his inspiration from the Pauline idea of the 'mystical body' of Christ,[7] which represents the most advanced development of the idea of the 'Kingdom of God', going quite clearly beyond 'organisation' to the higher unity of an *organism*.

Teilhard finds in nature, unfolding itself in evolution, a strong basis for the astounding concept of an organic unity between Christ and individual believers. Studying the history of organic evolution we find one pervasive and paradoxical law: 'unity differentiates'; in other words, the higher stages of organic unity always bring with them greater and greater differentiation. In Teilhard's view this applies also to social and cultural evolution, which will eventually culminate in a 'collective consciousness', which will cover the earth with a sheathing of thought, 'the noosphere', in which maximum individualisation and personalisation will be compatible with the ultimate unity of a super-organism.[8] The natural processes of evolution, which will inevitably and ultimately bring about this state, are now under the direction of the Christ who has immersed himself in matter; and these processes may also be assisted, facilitated and accelerated by human co-operation. The 'collective consciousness' which will result will be a state of religious correlativism. Religious or mystical experience, which was formerly an exceptional happening, because it was simply an anomalous foretaste of what would be the common experience under the collective consciousness, will no longer be individualistic but a shared experience; and the collective consciousness which is produced (the human counterpart of divine life)[9], far from extinguishing individuality, as happens in mass collective movements like communism, will augment individuality and individual spiritual perfection to the highest possible extent. The individual pursuit of religious perfection and the experience of religious communion will be no longer distinguishable phenomena, but inseparable reciprocals.

In conclusion, the approach utilised by religion to overcome or obviate the alienations conditioned by morality can be summarily schematised as follows:

| *Subjective dispositions* | *Objective norms* |
| --- | --- |

### *Traditional religion*

| | |
| --- | --- |
| The attainment of a state of unity with God, who brings harmony to the soul, and leads one spontaneously to go beyond the requirements of duty, thus avoiding all guilt and alienation caused by conflict between inclination and duty. | An ecumenical community, dedicated to the preservation and further development of a non-alienated organisation, based on love and similarity of beliefs and religious practices. |

### *Correlativistic religion (Teilhard)*

| | |
| --- | --- |
| Attainment of the highest state of individuality by union with the spirit animating the evolving mystical body of Christ. | A collective consciousness produced as an offshoot of individual convergent consciousnesses, and guaranteeing the further evolutionary development of these consciousnesses. |

## 4(b)   THE COMMON GOOD

The 'common good' in the English language has some conceptual affinity with 'common weal' and 'common wealth', and obviously refers to some benefit which many share in common. But beyond this common-denominator meaning, it has various specific connotations, depending on the context in which it is used. Politicians pride themselves on working for the common good; laws are supposed to be conducive to the common good; and economic practices are also thought to promote the common good. Thus the common good can be conveniently subdivided into at least three spheres: political, legal and economic. Each of these spheres involves a reciprocity of individual need-fulfilment and public unification and order, which can be expressed schematically as follows, with regard to each of the three spheres:

## THE COMMON GOOD

|  | Individual need-fulfilment | Public unification and order |
|---|---|---|
| The political aspect of the common good | There must be input from and recognition of, all individuals of the polity in some institutionalised way. The wishes of the governed must be heard, and taken into account, by those governing. The optimum state of affairs (pure democracy) would obtain when the governed are actually their own governors. | Public order, authority, welfare and protection, must be maintained, on both national and local levels, by officials who reflect the desires of the people and who may even (in a pure democracy, and presumably on a small scale) be identical with the people. |
| The legal aspect of the common good | There should be legal recognition of individual rights, based on needs, and on desires which do not conflict unreasonably with the desires of others. | Civil and criminal legislation should be sufficiently extensive to maintain public order, but overlegislation, duplication of laws, and obsolete laws should be avoided. |
| The economic aspect of the common good | Capitalistic competition in a free market. Reasonable opportunities for profit maximisation. Reasonable incentives to ensure industry and ingenuity. | Governmental regulation to insure against trusts in restraint of trade, price fixing, unfair business practices, pollution of the environment; and to help maintain minimal standards of living when private efforts are unable to do so. |

By thus dividing the amalgamous 'common good' into its various spheres and aspects, we are better enabled to appreciate what is concretely implied by the concept: in the political sphere, the common good consists in avoiding extremes of anarchy and totalitarianism, in creating an orderly government with maximum participation of the governed; in the legal sphere, it lies somewhere between the extremes of litigiousness on the part of individuals and overlegislation on the part of government; in the economic sphere, somewhere between ruthless *laissez-faire* capitalism and mono-polistic state control of the entire economy. We in the capitalist world like to think that our 'liberal democracy' is the only form of government that can insure the common good in all of its spheres and aspects; but it is not inconceivable that, with some modifications, communist constitutions might be able to equal or surpass us in their achievement of the common good, which achievement is always an approximation in any case.[10]

It should be obvious that conceptions of the common good will often intersect with moral theories, and vice versa, A utilitarian and a Marxist, for example, are very likely to have different ideas of what constitutes the common good, based on a difference of emphasis. And Sartre and Aristotle's differing conceptions of the common good are not unconnected with their ethical theories.

Having sketched out the salient differences between moral good and other species of good – religious and aesthetic, as well as the 'common' good – I am in a position now to attempt a more intensive analysis and definition of the moral good in Chapter 5. Then, in Chapter 6, I shall focus on areas of interconnection and interface – certain problematic practical intersections of moral values and the other species of value which seem to be in particular need of clarification in the contemporary world.

# 5

# The Fully Differentiated Moral Good

## ARGUMENT

*Having at this point differentiated the moral good as far as possible from other 'species' of good, we examine both philosophical theories concerning morality and a widespread moral code – the Ten Commandments – in search of some 'common denominator' feature or features. One interesting characteristic that turns up is a common concern with the negative parameters, the outer limits, of human behaviour, and a notable reluctance to make specific positive rules to govern decision-making well within those parameters.*

---

## 5(a)  THE NATURE OF ETHICAL THEORIES

Even in the physical sciences there seems to be some equivocation in the use of the word 'theory'. Sometimes 'theory' means (a) a simple *hypothesis* explaining certain phenomenal events, for example Mendel's hypothesis about the genetic transmission of dominant and recessive inherited characteristics; sometimes the term is used to designate (b) a 'law', that is, a hypothesis which has received final, precise formulation and been so fully verified that it is no longer *just* a hypothesis (an example would be Mendel's law in the twentieth century, after it had been confirmed by repeated experiments, by visual evidence from electron microscopes, etc.); but in a more fundamental sense, the same term is used to refer to (c) a very general formulation or formula about the overarching structures or dynamics of physical reality, in the context of which the various scientific 'hypotheses' or 'laws' have their intelligibility (for example, the theory of evolution provides an overall *general* framework from which specific laws like Mendel's law take their context). In a less proper sense (d) technology might be said to involve 'theories' in so far as it stimulates the formulation of certain hypotheses concerning the functioning, or the best possible functioning of natural or mechanical or cybernetic systems, in accordance with certain scientific theories which they presuppose. For example, I might speak not inappropriately about my 'theory' concerning the best possible way of producing sturdy but edible hybrids of vegetables in a certain climate, or of achieving maximum fuel efficiency in gasoline combustion engines, or of securing computer systems with sensitive or classified data from infiltration by unauthorised users. In such cases I would be 'theorising' in a technological context which presupposes certain scientific (biological or physical or cybernetic) theories.

Ethical theories are commonly subdivided into descriptive, normative and meta-ethical theories. There is a sense in which descriptive and meta-ethical theories are 'scientific' in a straightforward empirical way. Descriptive theories, which purport to characterise the values or norms to which people or societies actually adhere, might be considered hypotheses which can be confirmed or falsified by observation, opinion polls, psychological testing, etc. Meta-ethical theories, which are concerned with the analysis and interpretation of ethical language, may be considered scientific hypotheses in a broader sense, *if* we allow that there are certain established scientific methods for analysing language (a claim that would certainly be allowed by some linguists, scholars in biblical hermeneutics, and literary critics, although there are considerable verification problems connected with this type of 'hypothesis').

John Dewey was somewhat unusual among ethicists in claiming that *normative* ethical theories – theories prescribing behaviour – should be 'hypotheses' in more or less the same sense as hypotheses in the physical sciences (he seems to have in mind especially sense (a) discussed above). In the 'scientific' system of morals which he championed, there are no fixed or stable values, and 'a purpose is held only as a working hypothesis until results confirm its rightness'.[1] In such a system, 'no individual or group will be judged by whether they come up to or fall short of some fixed result, but by the direction in which they are moving'.[2] Dewey's theory (portrayed as an extension of evolutionary theory) depicts human growth as a broadly-based cultural and social improvement. In line with his correlative approach to ethics (see pp. 92–3 above) it prescribes an awareness of natural and social evolution, and a suitable response, conditioned and facilitated by liberal democratic institutions and mores, which will produce individual moral growth.[3]

Dewey's claim makes the most sense, however, if we understand it *not* in terms of an analogy with the physical sciences proper, but in terms of an analogy with the 'technological' model mentioned above.[4] Dewey's theory and the other normative theories we have considered in Chapter 3 are, explicitly or implicitly, practical rules of a very general nature, or constellations of such practical rules, concerned with promoting morally right dispositions and/or behaviour. Although they are commonly called 'theories', it is not accurate to call them 'theories' at all, just as it would not be accurate to call technology 'science'. They are most similar to 'theories' concerned with technological operations (sense (d) above) – operations which are based on certain scientific theories in the strict sense. (*In what follows, the use of inverted commas for 'theory' will indicate this extended, less strict usage.*)

The normative ethicist expounds 'theories' concerned with proper human behaviour, which 'theories' are based on certain philosophical theories (not scientific hypotheses but philosophical insights, the verification or falsification of which is on a very abstract and subjective level). For example, Kant's first formulation of the categorical imperative[5] is a practical 'theory' based on a theory concerning human nature – the theory that non-self-contradiction and the power of universalisation are essential differentiating characteristics of rational beings. And, in general, all the various moral approaches or normative 'theories' we have considered are based on philosophical theories concerning the prime attribute or attributes of human nature, the ultimate teleology of social life, or the teleology of nature and human nature.

Some further examples: Sartre's 'theory' of 'good faith' is based on the rather paradoxical theory that the fundamental attribute of human nature is to have no nature, that is, to be completely free, determined not by 'nature' in *any* sense, but by oneself. Bentham's 'theory' of utilitarianism is based on the enlightened and progressive philosophical social-political theory that the teleology of individual behaviour is to contribute to the happiness and welfare of the maximum number of persons. The Thomistic 'theory' of natural law is based on a broad Aristotelian theory about the teleology of nature and human nature, encompassing such things as self-preservation, reproduction of the species, proper rearing and education of offspring, etc. The Stoic 'natural law' 'theory', on the other hand, is based on the monistic Stoic cosmological theory, according to which the teleology of nature and human nature is to carry out the will of God, whose spirit or law permeates and guides all the world, including the social world. And Marx's paradoxically moral 'theory' concerning the necessity of overthrowing capitalism and its bourgeois 'morality', is based on the teleology of his theory of historical materialism, which he claimed to be a truly scientific interpretation of the natural history of economic–social–political formations.

Could we speak of a 'result' of applying such theories? The result could not be anything so concrete and measurable as producing sturdier vegetables, or increasing fuel efficiency, or preventing security lapses (to continue with the technological analogies introduced above). A *positive* result of the practical application of an ethical 'theory' would arguably be related to some real or perceived increase of the elusive and unstable quality of human happiness – even if that happiness consists, as for the Kantian, in the assurance that one has acted without regard for, and even in apparent opposition to, one's 'happiness'; or consists in the assurance that virtue is its own reward, or in the assurance that moral commitment to duty has freed the individual from any demeaning dependence on 'results'. Such paradoxes are much easier to avoid in discussions of technology than in discussions of human behaviour.

## 5(b)  THE NATURE OF THE MORALLY GOOD

As we saw in our treatment of the normative theories discussed in Chapter 3, some of them emphasise subjective aspects, others objective aspects. This emphasis can be carried to an extreme, resulting in a one-sided, deficient, incomplete concept of moral good. Because of this possibility, it might be most conducive to a complete and integral conception of the morally good if some sort of metaphilosophical testing *of the theories* took place. For example, if the utilitarian Nazis, who wanted to eliminate Jews to attain the greatest happiness of the German majority, had tested their objectives against Kant's categorical imperative (*second* formulation), they could have avoided an extreme and simplistic application of the utilitarian philosophy; if the Marxists who advocate 'expropriating the expropriators' were to apply Kant's categorical imperative (*first* formulation), they might have some second thoughts when they considered the fact that, as expropriators themselves, they should be subject to the same law; and the judge who hesitates about punishing a murderer, because of the Golden Rule (to use Kant's example),[6] might overcome his hesitation if he were to refer to the unequivocal prohibition of murder in the natural law. It would seem that Sartre himself was conducting some such test, in his efforts to come to an accommodation with Marxism, which he considered the *de facto* chief source for *objective* norms in the modern world; and it might be claimed that Sartrean existentialism gained by this accommodation an enhanced awareness of social responsibility, while Marxism gained by becoming considerably more elastic than its rigid, doctrinaire 'economism' had allowed.[7] If Sartre himself, however, in his intermittent advocacy of revolutionary terrorism had tested this terrorist 'expression of freedom' against the Stoic emphasis on the importance of furthering the harmony of man with nature, and man with man, some of the more brutal implications of Sartre's revolutionary existentialism might have been mitigated.

The correlative approaches discussed earlier[8] may more easily avoid one-sided extremes, albeit at the expense of *specificity*. Hegel's correlativism of rights and duties in the state and in the individual, for example, is oriented towards promoting a general attitude, but would be difficult to apply to specific cases in which there is a conflict between rights or duties; and Dewey's correlativism of individual, social and environmental evolution is a very general world view which is often unconvincing when it comes to details about what this growth actually entails.

But we should not expect too much from the theorists. The moral good is to be found only in actual practice, and moral theories can only point the way towards the good, thus possibly aiding in its recognition when it comes to pass. What, then, *do* the theories tell us? And how *do* we recognise the moral good? An analogy based on electrical polarity may be of assistance here. Positive and negative electric potential will not produce usable electricity until the circuit is closed, producing an electrical current. So also in ethics the relevant 'potential' can be broken down into a combination of some expressed or implied insight about what is uniquely human, and some broad, overarching, non-provincial, objectively acceptable ways of expressing this uniqueness. When these two factors come together, then the 'circuit is closed', and moral good – which is neither an object, nor a property of an object, nor a subjective state – is produced.

If we would like to have *specific rules* concerning the moral good, we should first be forewarned by the example and experience of Socrates. The famous 'voice' or *'daimon'* which Socrates claimed to have possessed from childhood was an internal oracle of a strictly *negative* sort. It warned Socrates about what was evil or harmful, but never gave him any specific positive injunctions as to what he should *do*.[9] So also the strength of moral theories and of the moral rules derived from them consists not so much in giving us certain knowledge about what we should do, but in giving us some rather reliable guidelines as to what should be avoided. There are literally an infinite number of ways in which the moral person can accomplish positive moral good; and something like artistic ingenuity or creativity is required to discover them. There is also an infinity of ways in which an immoral person can accomplish evil. But for the moral person there are only a finite number of major 'points of no return' (or at least of difficult return) which must be avoided, if one is to stay within the general parameters of morality.

The various normative moral theories we have discussed in Chapter 3 have not always been assiduous in emphasising the strictly negative parameters. Although most formulations of the Golden Rule are negative in form, the Christian version is positive; although the applications Kant makes of the first formulation of the categorical imperative are negative, some of the applications he makes of the second formulation are positive; Adam Smith's 'Impartial Spectator' test can be used either to test what sort of actions we have a repulsion for, or to test for positive features; the utilitarian formula can be applied either to the minimisation of suffering and pain, or to the maximisation of pleasure or happiness. But in any case these theories generally avoid getting too specific about positive rules for behaviour; and the mistakes attributed to the theorisers – for example, Kant's mistake in regard to the permissibility of lying to save another's life, Aquinas's mistake regarding the permissibility of slavery, Sartre's mistake in advocating terrorism as a means of liberation – can best be understood as faulty specifications which do not necessarily invalidate the general principles on which they are based. The *main* contribution of normative moral theories is to define negative parameters and indirectly a positive overall context, the knowledge of which will help one to achieve and actually create the moral good in specific ways. If we were to sum up the thrust of all such theories in one very general meta-principle, this latter would simply explicate the final thrust of the 'electrical polarity' analogy discussed above: the moral good consists, subjectively, in the affirmation of the highest human qualities without infringing on the rights of others; objectively, in conformity with nature and/or with the more universal standards of social harmony which do not entail injustice to individuals or groups; and optimally, in unpredictable and not easily formulisable ways of co-ordinating both these aspects.

## 5(c)  APPENDIX: THE DECALOGUE AS A CASE STUDY

In Judaeo-Christian culture, the Ten Commandments may be taken as an interesting example of a moral code which (in accord with the pattern adumbrated above) concentrates explicitly on the negative parameters of human behaviour (although some positive general guidelines are also implicit), and avoids the perils of detailing rules governing specific positive duties.

The Ten Commandments said to be given by God to his people through Moses in Exodus 20: 2–17 have been subjected to various formulations and numberings by Jews, Catholics, Protestants and Orthodox Christians. I shall follow the formulation given by Harrelson,[10] which is a slightly revised version of Nielson's formulation.[11] Harrelson's English formulation reads as follows:

1. Thou shalt not have other gods.
2. Thou shalt not make for thyself an idol.
3. Thou shalt not lift up the name of Yahweh for mischief (or Nielson: 'take the name of Yahweh in vain').
4. Thou shalt not treat with contempt the sabbath day.
5. Thou shalt not curse thy father or thy mother.
6. Thou shalt not kill thy neighbour.
7. Thou shalt not commit adultery with the wife of thy neighbour.
8. Thou shalt not steal anything that is thy neighbour's.
9. Thou shalt not answer thy neighbour as a false witness (or Nielson: 'bear false witness against thy neighbour').
10. Thou shalt not covet the household of thy neighbour.

It might appear at first sight that the first four commandments have no direct relevance for ethics; but Harrelson finds, alongside the more overt religious meanings, significant ethical meanings:[12] 'Thou shalt not have other gods' implies a unity of life and endeavour, an avoidance of dualism in thought or practice; 'thou shalt not make for thyself an idol' has to be taken in the context of the biblical idea that the true 'image of God' is *man*, and *human community* – which should be the main objects of our ethical focus; 'thou shalt not take the name of Yahweh in vain' means that we should not use God or religion to gain some excess of power over others; and 'thou shalt not treat with contempt the sabbath day', standing in contrast to the 'work ethic', enjoins us to spend some time 'doing nothing', cultivating family relationships, etc. (It is noteworthy, says Harrelson,[13] that no 'religious' duties are prescribed on the Sabbath.)

But it is, of course, the last six commandments whose moral relevance is most explicit. These commandments simply define the outer parameters of the morally good, beyond which there is little hope of benefiting ourselves or society, but within which there is the possibility of self-acceptance and recognition by others, and an endless variety of interpretations and applications: the fifth commandment, 'thou shalt not curse thy father or thy mother' forbids neglect of, and disrespect for, elderly parents, and, by extension (in our less family-oriented society) the retired and elderly in general. The sixth commandment, 'thou shalt not kill thy neighbour', establishes the absolute 'bottom line' with regard to killing. Possibly every human being short of an enemy might be included in the term 'neighbour' – any inclusion, in the interests of pacifism, of absolute enemies would force the idea beyond its natural limits. The seventh commandment, 'thou shalt not commit adultery . . .', specifies 'the wife of thy neighbour'. The Bible elsewhere clearly prohibits fornication and other sexual sins, but the prohibition of adultery which affects families and society in general, is characterised as a prohibition from which there can be no 'situational' exceptions. The eighth commandment, 'thou shalt not steal . . .', according to Harrelson,[14] prohibits by implication any actions, for example, pollution of the earth or exorbitant deficit spending, that would cause serious diminishment of the basic life-goods of others (including future generations). The ninth commandment, 'thou shalt not answer thy neighbour as a false witness', is particularly concerned with official statements and contractual commitments, not with the lesser varieties of lies, dishonesty, and cheating. The tenth commandment, 'thou shalt not covet the household of thy neighbour', is of particular interest because it is concerned not with any overt act, but with something we would characterise as 'subjective' – a desire; it places an absolute limit on desiring what another possesses. And some would say that the other nine commandments are also concerned at least in part with intentions.[15]

It is to be noted that it would be possible for individuals to be involved in lying, dishonesty, sexual offences of various sorts, even unscrupulous profit-making, and other types of arguably questionable activity, without blatantly breaking any of the Ten Commandments. This is because the Ten Commandments are concerned only with establishing the absolute parameters, beyond which one can no longer be considered a member of the moral community. As shown in Figure 3, we could portray these absolute parameters as the outer limits of a circle, circumscribing the sphere of 'moral good'.

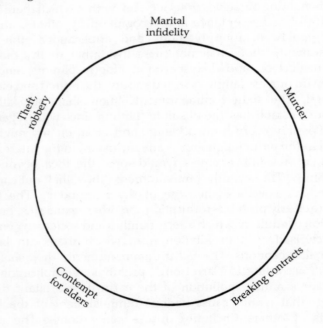

**Figure 3**

The 'moral good', by implication, is somewhere within these parameters – preferably well within, but also possibly to some extent in the borderline or fringe areas. And the moral good would consist in the endless variety of ways in which one might foster his or her own life, property and associations without infringing, even through 'covetousness', on those of others. The Decalogue thus avoids that specification of a multiplicity of positive rules for moral good which would interfere with the situational encounter between human ingenuity and objective requirements that is, as we saw, of the essence for the creation of moral good.

# 6

# Interconnections

## ARGUMENT

*The differentiation of moral and other types of good is not just a theoretical pursuit relevant to the arcane sphere of 'axiology', but has practical implications. In fact, it seems that some of the major moral issues of our day involve an intersection and sometimes a confusion of moral good with the other types of good, or vice versa. We turn then, finally to some contemporary moral issues to illustrate ways in which they may possibly be clarified, if not solved, by a recognition of the convergence and possible confusion of the above-mentioned species of good.*

Having defined moral good and differentiated it from aesthetic and religious good, and from 'the common good' in some of its connotations, I shall give some consideration finally to some of the areas of interconnection between moral good and the other species of good. After drawing attention to the most salient *divergences* in four major interfaces of morality with other areas, I shall concentrate on some of the more important areas where there is a *subjunction* (morality subjoined to another area, or another area subjoined to morality), and also on some contemporary ethical problem areas which exemplify *'category mistakes'*. The term 'category mistake' was coined by Gilbert Ryle to designate the sort of confusion that results when a thing or aspect that belongs in one category is treated as if it belonged in another very different category. Ryle's primary application of the idea of a 'category mistake' was to the mind-body relationship, insofar as the mind and its operations are sometimes spoken of as if they were just like the body and its operations – which is to place the mind in the wrong category. But my prime concern here will be with some controversial issues in which a certain confusion of moral categories with other categories seems to perpetuate and exacerbate the controversy.[1]

## 6(a)   ETHICS AND AESTHETICS

### 6(a) 1.   Divergences

'Aesthetics', in the wide sense in which I have been using the term, is oriented towards immediate, 'first-order' enjoyment, fulfilment of inclinations, active and passive aesthetic experience, actions in accord with dispositions and in accord with one's surroundings. Ethics, in contrast, is oriented towards reflective, second-order satisfaction, in which inclination is secondary to acting in accordance with what is highest in oneself, and/or with certain fundamental objective moral norms.

### 6(a) 2.   Subjunctions

*6(a) 2.1.   The Subjunction of Aesthetics to Morality*
The annexation of aesthetics as a sort of appendage to ethics takes its more grossly obvious form in censorship on the basis of purely *moral* considerations, as contradistinguished (a) from psychological considerations (for example, the suitability of certain materials for young or immature audiences), and (b) from strictly aesthetic considerations (for example, the determination that anything startlingly ugly or offensive should be kept out of public places). A similar subjunction is discernible in the attempt to utilise art as a merely attractive vehicle for moral ideology, as exemplified in the periodic tight control exerted by the Soviet Union over its art and literature, or, on a more individual basis in the work of novelists (such as Henry James, Saul Bellow, Albert Camus, George Orwell and Ayn Rand) who use fiction as a means of conveying a moral message. But an overly strict subjection of aesthetics to the control of ethics quashes spontaneity and originality, and thus has the paradoxical effect of eliminating the truly aesthetic elements altogether.

A more moderate subjunction than censorship would be the intentional and planned expansion of an autonomous and self-sufficient aesthetics in order to produce some presumed indirect and unpredictable but beneficial effect on morals.[2] This recommendation avoids the paradoxical extermination of aesthetics by the ethics it is supposed to serve, while maintaining some minimal subordination of aesthetics to ethics.

*6(a) 2.2.   The Subjunction of Ethics to Aesthetics*

A prime area in which aesthetics has, or should have, an overarching influence on ethics is with regard to hedonistic utilitarianism, which is oriented towards maximising 'non-moral' good, that is, aesthetic satisfaction (again, in the broad sense in which I have been using the term 'aesthetic'). For the conception of this non-moral good will presumably affect the character of all utilitarian calculations and strivings. The 'non-moral' good may be conceived, for example, as bare survival, or as gaudy luxury, or as comfortable middle-class existence, or as a richly diversified community experience, or as utopia. The utilitarian formula, 'the greatest happiness of the greatest number', is remarkably defective in clarity and concreteness. The content of this purely formal idea for a utilitarian hedonist must ultimately come from an aesthetic conception, which will largely dictate the subsequent direction of the utilitarian reasoning involved.[3]

## 6(a) 3.   Category Mistakes

*6(a) 3.1.   Homophilia*

Homosexuality was thought in times past to be a psychological aberration or possibly even a symptom of moral perversity. More recent research[4] has indicated a definite genetic and/or hormonal basis for homosexuality in both sexes. If this is indeed the case, homosexual attraction is largely or fundamentally an 'aesthetic' matter, and reactions against homosexuals on the part of heterosexuals are also attributable to their own aesthetic orientation (which renders homosexuality aesthetically repugnant). In other words, both the sexual orientation of homosexuals and the repugnance to homosexuality on the part of heterosexuals is something largely outside the realm of rational or moral control. If homosexuality is either (a) glorified by homosexuals as a higher and more noble state, or (b) denigrated by heterosexuals as a moral perversion, a category mistake would seem to be made. To be sure, aesthetic orientations are important in human associations, but to attach moral judgements unnecessarily to these orientations is seriously to misinterpret them and overload the moral 'docket', so to speak.

*6(a) 3.2.   Racial, Ethnic and National Characteristics*

No doubt much of the prejudice extant in our world has taken its inception from aesthetic judgements. One begins with an unfavourable judgement about habits of personal cleanliness, upkeep of property, speech mannerisms, style of life, facial characteristics, eating habits, external religious rituals, etc. – and gradually and unconsciously potentiates these aesthetic judgements into judgements about the basic moral worth of a group of people. Avoidance of such a category mistake will not automatically change one's tastes, but should help to mitigate in many cases the more vicious aspects of prejudice which result from the sense of moral superiority of the prejudiced person.

### 6(a) 3.3.  *Pornography*
Although it is difficult to define pornography, most people are able to discern the difference between a tasteful, empathetic, artistic or photographic depiction of a nude subject, and the prurient, loveless preoccupation with depersonalised nakedness which is a hallmark of pornography. 'Hard core' pornography is simply pornography in which this difference has become most obvious. The category mistake most frequent in regard to pornography seems to be the reverse of the types of mistakes just discussed; in other words, it is a mistaken assignment of an aesthetic category to an ethical issue, rather than vice versa. Pornography is definitely an ethical issue, if one subscribes to the basic ethical principle that a person is never to be used merely as an object. In its extreme manifestations it has involved the exploitation of children and teenagers, the unnatural photographic depiction of torsos without heads, even the graphically portrayed sadistic torturing and murder of the photographic subject. But even in its less extreme forms it involves the use of a person reduced to a pure object (often through a depiction of poses reminiscent of animal mating 'display' rituals) for the purposes of mere sexual arousal. And so those who defend pornography as a kind of 'lowest common denominator' aesthetic experience, which is permissible as long as 'community standards of taste' (to use the US Supreme Court's definition) are met, are making a serious category mistake. And if Susan Griffin is correct, pornography is not only not art, but is the antithesis of, and an affront to, the genuinely aesthetic. For it is the product of a culture which is determined to achieve mastery over nature, and over woman as a symbol of nature, and over the spontaneous sensations and feelings which the beauty of woman arouses in a man – sensations and feelings which he wants to have the power of arousing in himself without admitting any subjection or

responsibilities to the woman whom he uses for arousal.[5] The result
is the paradoxical deadening even of the erotic, which in its
authentic aesthetic expression is dependent on personal
relationships and the surprises and gradual revelations which the
latter can bring about. But the pornographer fears the *personal* above
all. 'Just as the sadomasochist tells us he seeks feeling, when indeed
he is afraid of feeling, so also the pornographer, who says he would
bring sexuality into consciousness, . . . in fact wishes to suppress
and silence sexual knowledge.'[6]

### 6(a) 3.4.   *Cohabitation*

The noted philosopher Bertrand Russell summed up the anti-
Victorian mood of the 1920s when he wrote, in *Marriage and Morals*,[7]
'It seems absurd to ask people to enter upon a relation intended to be
lifelong, without any previous knowledge as to their sexual
compatibility.' Russell's recommendation was for short-term
relationships which might lead to marriage and children, if the
couples found themselves to be sexually compatible. The reasoning
behind Russell's recommendations – which has elicited agreement
from a rather large number of philosophers – is aesthetic in nature:
how can an individual assure aesthetic compatibility, especially in
sex (which is thought to be one of the most intense pleasures),
without actual sexual experience and experimentation? Evidence
from the Kinsey Reports and elsewhere indicates that a good
majority of people have followed Russell's advice up to the present
time. The results have not been encouraging, if divorce statistics are
any indication. In recent decades, approximately half the marriages
in the United States have ended in divorce – a marked increase over
earlier statistics. A similar increase in divorces has been noticeable in
many European countries. One cause, among others, for this
increase seems to be that a very basic category mistake has been
made. Marriage – especially in Western cultures in which the main
objective of marriage is the development of a lifelong *personal*
relationship as well as the rearing of children, and not just
satisfaction of the sexual drive – is primarily an ethical relationship.
The expectation is that one's spouse will also be a close friend, or
even one's best friend, sharing one's values, and mature enough to
make a stable commitment. Concentration on the aesthetic aspects,
such as sexual compatibility, will give one little or no evidence of
ethical compatibility, and may even militate against the objective
assessment of such compatibility, resulting in the marriages of

couples who are antagonistic regarding basic values, intellectually and/or psychologically incompatible, and possibly unable to communicate or collaborate in ordinary tasks, including the task of raising children. If a couple were certain of basic ethical compatibility, then a 'companionate' or 'trial' marriage might help to give them information about their sexual compatibility, if they were in doubt. But if they are 'living together', without strong prior friendship ties, with the end in view of deciding on ethical compatibility (which is much more complex than sexual compatibility), the odds are unfortunately against them, especially if a protracted period of cohabitation restricts contacts and dating with others of the opposite sex. And so 'living together' often seems to involve a category mistake – making aesthetic compatibility primary, rather than ethical compatibility and friendship. There is no guarantee that avoidance of this category mistake will lead to happier marriages; it is not impossible that those who place the emphasis on aesthetic compatibility will also achieve ethical compatibility; and if one does not have any strong need or expectation of lasting ethical commitment in marriage, he or she can easily avoid this category mistake. But for those who *do* have such a need or expectation, avoidance of the category mistake would help assure consistency and correspondence between one's attitudes towards dating and courtship and his or her attitudes towards marriage – and this should be a considerable benefit in modern Western society.

## 6(b)   MORALITY AND RELIGION

### 6(b) 1.   Divergences

The major religions of the world have often been allied with a moral code – an example would be the alignment of the Judaeo-Christian tradition with the Ten Commandments – and sometimes, as we noted above,[8] even with a particular moral theory. But, as we have seen,[9] the distinctive characteristic of the major religions is not their moral code (if they have one), but their orientation towards going beyond morality and its inevitable frustrations and alienations to some ideal of personal and/or communal perfection – an ideal which elicits such a singleness of purpose and spiritual power that the religious individual hopes to place himself beyond the confines of merely moral considerations and calculations.

## 6(b) 2.  Subjunctions

### *6(b) 2.1.  The Subjunction of Religion to Morality*

If indeed religion strives to go beyond morality, it should not expect therewith to be also beyond subjection to at least minimal standards of morality. In the Judaeo-Christian tradition, the example of Abraham, who was commanded by God to slay his son Isaac and then was given a last-minute reprieve from carrying out the slaughter, has often been taken as an indication that religious inspiration is not judged by moral norms;[10] but Abraham's last-minute reprieve may equally be taken as an indication that morality won out in this case (Abraham lived in an era in which human sacrifice was practised) and should win out in similar cases. In the Roman Catholic Church, a number of important policy decisions seem to have resulted primarily from moral considerations: the law of clerical celibacy, which became finalised in the twelfth century in the First and Second Lateran Councils, seemed to be at least partly a reaction to practices of nepotism, especially as regards inheritances and appointments in the upper echelons of the ecclesiastical hierarchy; the Crusades' campaigns of extermination and the Inquisition's executions were eventually abandoned and abhorred, partly for moral reasons; slavery, as has been noted above,[11] was eventually condemned in the nineteenth century for moral reasons; and the strong contemporary papal opposition to participation in politics by priests and nuns in Latin America and elsewhere seems to stem from some long-standing memories of the moral corruption which resulted from the joining of religion and politics in past centuries. In the much less centralised Protestant church, 'official' doctrinal positions have been of lesser importance. Yet, without any real necessity for official proclamations, practices such as the persecution of Jews and Catholics, the burning of witches, etc., have gradually become subject to overwhelming disapproval among Protestants on moral grounds. Likewise, in Mormonism the abolition of polygamy, in some Islamic countries the abolition of discrimination against women and excessively savage forms of punishment, and in Hinduism the official (but not yet practically implemented) condemnation of the caste system and wife-burning, have resulted from moral pressures from inside and outside the religious community.

*6(b) 2.2.   The Subjunction of Morality to Religion*

Morality for the most part is concerned with minimal standards of behaviour, that is, the basic duties and responsibilities which a human being has to himself and others. Religion, at its furthest reaches, promulgates maximal standards – for example, the injunction in the Christian religion to love all men, including one's enemies. Freud criticises this latter injunction as amounting to a dilution of love (through overextension), impossible of fulfilment, and even morally wrong (since it does not take into account the worthiness of the person to be loved).[12] But it may be argued against Freud that it is precisely the tendency of such 'supererogatory' religious commands to go beyond the minimal standards of morality which supplies an indispensable check on morality and a productive incentive towards self-criticism. This function becomes evident, for example, if we compare Christian universalism to utilitarianism, whose implicit tendencies towards majoritarianism could on some interpretations lead, as we saw, to conclusions compromising the rights of minorities.

## 6(b) 3.   Category Mistakes

*6(b) 3.1.   Contraception*

In Pope Paul VI's encyclical letter, *Humanae vitae*, the strong condemnation of artificial contraception (that is, of all forms of birth control except the 'safe period' method) is based primarily on ethical arguments (derived from the Thomistic concept of the 'natural law') and secondarily on a religious argument. The core of the religious argument is to be found towards the end of the encyclical:

> To dominate instinct by means of one's reason and free will undoubtedly require ascetical practices, so that the affective manifestations of conjugal life may observe the correct order, in particular with regard to the observance of periodic continence.[13]

In this latter passage the Pope is 'wearing another hat'. He is not appealing to a natural law or any other ethical principle, but to traditional religious principles, which state that ascetical practices are required in order to attain that unity of instinct, reason and will which will put one beyond the pale of pedestrian moral conflicts. Not only Catholicism, but also Hinduism and Buddhism have recommended sexual asceticism, even celibacy, as a means to attaining that transcendent unity and harmony of personality which is the goal of all major religions. The *religious* message of the Pope's encyclical is that the use of artificial means to avoid the natural, procreation-oriented rhythms of sexual fertility is a form of hedonistic indulgence which is antithetical to the attainment of personal spiritual perfection.

But this religious message carries no 'clout'. It is simply a recommendation of a form of voluntary asceticism in regard to sexual intercourse. On the other hand, the appeal to the 'natural law', as an arbiter of one's duty in this regard, gives 'clout' to the message, makes it into a *law* for everyone. It is to be feared, however, that the intermingling of an alleged strict moral law with the supererogatory religious counsel weakens the effect of both. In any case, the effect of the religious message seems to be lost on the person it is intended to reach – the genuinely religious person who presumably might be persuaded that he should adopt this form of asceticism along with others he is already committed to. The rather controversial applicability of the 'natural law' (is the primary natural teleology or purpose of sexual intercourse for *human beings* really procreation, and the expression and confirmation of the bonds of affection only a secondary purpose?) makes it doubly important that the religious considerations, which transcend natural law, are spelled out clearly. But the category mistake of presenting a strong religious recommendation as an absolute moral imperative makes this goal difficult to achieve.

### 6(b) 3.2.   *Conscientious Objection*

It is not to be doubted that those who claim exemption from military service because of conscientious objections are sometimes merely draft evaders who are motivated primarily by laziness, indifference, etc. But those who have genuine *moral* objections to participation in a war may find it difficult, if not impossible, to establish their case unless they appeal to a religious motivation. Draft boards which make decisions on these cases generally look for long-standing religious traditions which can be appealed to in justification of a pacifist stance. For a Christian, having been a Quaker or Jehovah's Witness for some time helps considerably to establish one's case. But there is also a pacifist tradition in mainline Catholicism and Protestantism which can be appealed to by the religious conscientious objector. What is difficult to appeal to legally is an affiliation with a non-religious peace movement; and it is even more difficult to appeal to a personal, once-in-a-lifetime moral decision. Thus, by a process of forfeit, conscientious objectors are often constrained to place their strictly *moral* objections into a *religious* category. This category mistake becomes particularly rampant during times of wholesale military combat and involuntary conscription, and perpetuates a conventional deceit whose existence is ironically recognised by both the deceiver and the deceived.

## 6(c)  MORALITY AND POLITICS

### 6(c) 1.  Divergences

In regard to the question concerning the proper relationship between morality and politics, a great disparity of interpretations has arisen in the history of philosophy: from Aristotle's *Nicomachean Ethics*, in which ethics is presented as a branch of politics; to Machiavelli's *The Prince*, in which politics is divorced from morality; to Hobbes's *Leviathan*, in which the political is equated with the moral; to Kant's *Perpetual Peace*, in which the moral is the essential foundation for the political; to Hegel's *Philosophy of Right*, in which the political is the ultimate mature expression of the moral. If one concentrates only on contemporary Western liberal democracies, it is evident that politics, while not indifferent to morality, is primarily concerned with public order and safety and the protection of freedom. Within these parameters, politics can absorb and tolerate a great deal of private and even public immorality, depending on the threshold of sensitivity of the citizens. Thus politics diverges from morality insofar as it is concerned not with morality *per se*, but only with morality in so far as it is relevant to certain agreed-upon concepts of public order and public welfare. Outside the ambit of the Western democracies there are, of course, cultures or social systems which do not accept the distinction we take for granted between the 'private' and the 'public' domain, between individual conscience and laws enacted for public welfare. There can be no doubt that many international disputes now taking place regarding human rights, the moral validity of laws, etc., stem from some more fundamental differences of opinion concerning the parameters ascribable to morality and law, respectively.

## 6(c) 2.   Subjunctions

### *6(c) 2.1.   The Subjunction of Politics to Morality*

Although constitutional democracies in their everyday operations do not depend directly on any moral code or system, they are based fundamentally and historically on a judgement concerning the immorality not only of tyrannies and dictatorships, but also of absolute monarchies and autocracies, all of which are considered forms of mass exploitation and/or mass repression. It has also been claimed[14] that the three traditional signal political values of democracies – equality, liberty and fraternity – are entailed by the first, second and third formulations of Kant's categorical imperative, respectively. Whether or not this is the case, it does seem that in a general way the political value of equality is related to the rational emphasis on universality and self-consistency (manifested, for example, by the Golden Rule, as well as by Kant's first formulation); that the political commitment to liberty is related to the moral values of respect for persons and self-determination of persons; and that the political value of fraternity is related to the moral value of social consciousness. Communist systems, in so far as they are based on Marx's critique of bourgeois morality (see above, Chapter 3, section b[3]), would define not only their moral principles differently, but also their political values (for example, equality in terms of a classless society, liberty in terms of the freedom of workers from exploitation, etc.).

### *6(c) 2.2.   Subjunction of Morality to Politics*

Whether or not contemporary political systems, at least in their larger outlines, are originally based on certain definite moral presuppositions, there can be no doubt that they perceive themselves as perpetuating certain overarching moral values. Western democracy, even in its most socialist forms, takes special pride in the emphasis it places on respect for persons – a respect which is manifested not only by multiple intragovernmental safeguards for individual rights of citizens, but in intergovernmental campaigns and organisations concerned with the protection of human rights throughout the world.

The particular moral values which the Soviet government perceives itself to be perpetuating are well expressed in the following two excerpts, the first from a Soviet elementary school textbook, the second from a Soviet high school text.

Under communism each will receive not according to his work, but according to his needs. Thus, for example, in our country today everyone can already receive as much free medical care as is needed. All children are taught free of charge – all equally, whether their parents earn much or little.[15]

To the Soviet people, national egotism and chauvinism are alien. . . . In the future Communist society, all peoples of the world will stand as one friendly family. And then patriotism and internationalism will dissolve into one great feeling of love for all humanity and for its cradle – the planet Earth.[16]

There can be no doubt that the Soviets perceive themselves as perpetuating an advanced social consciousness reminiscent of Kant's 'Kingdom of Ends' (see above, Chapter 3, section a[4]) and an internationalism reminiscent of the Stoic vision of world citizenship. The social consciousness and internationalism associated with their communist vision is, of course, highly structured, controlled and administered at present by the interim 'representatives of the proletariat'. Such tight control is foreign to the Western mind, but may be acceptable and even attractive to those in the 'third' and 'fourth' worlds to whom survival through social solidarity is of greater urgency than considerations of liberty.

## 6(c) 3.  Category Mistakes

### 6(c) 3.1.  *The Right of National 'Self-Determination'*
The United States has in recent decades defended the right of self-determination of 'the people' in Chile, Vietnam, Nicaragua, and (somewhat selectively) elsewhere. In quite a few cases, some form of intervention, direct or indirect, has taken place. The reason given has been characterised as primarily a moral one; that is, our duty to defend this basic right, even where the right is not politically or legally guaranteed. But the actual situation sometimes belies these suppositions. For example, in the Vietnam of Ho Chi Minh and the Chile of Allende there did seem to be self-determination, if by 'self-determination' is meant the ratification of a leader, or even the ratifiability of a *de facto* leader, in a free election. The Nicaragua of Daniel Ortega might also turn out to be self-determined in this sense. It is simply a fact that the choice of the majority has sometimes been Marxism – a political system considered basically

incompatible with that of Western democracies, and a threat to the political self-determination of the people of America and other liberal democratic countries. Thus the more precise and complex meaning of our defence of self-determination in Vietnam and elsewhere, is that 'self-determination' to *communism*, because it is a threat to the self-determination of Western democracies, is an invalid form of self-determination (analogous to pursuing a right which infringes on the rights of others). There is some political basis for this paradoxical position in so far as the Marxism of Marx, Engels, Lenin and Stalin looked upon international expansion as necessary for the success of communism, and ultimate coexistence with capitalism as an impossibility. More recent statements from Soviet leaders have emphasised the possibility of the success of communism on national levels, and de-emphasised the necessity for engineering a worldwide revolution. If these latter statements can be taken seriously, there is less reason to oppose the self-determination of people to communism. But if there is evidence that the former bellicose position still prevails, there is a good political reason (self-preservation of national constitutional governments) for opposing even a 'self-determined' political process which leads to communism. In any case it is an over-simplification and a category mistake to confuse these political motivations with some morally motivated defence of the 'right to self-determination'.

## 6(c) 3.2.   *The Defensive Use of Nuclear Weaponry*
Even in an era in which it is generally agreed that a nuclear war would almost certainly result in 'mutually assured destruction' for both attacker and attacked, military strategists and politicians still sometimes emphasise the distinction to be made between the offensive and defensive use of nuclear weapons, and between a limited and a wholesale, injudicious defensive use of nuclear weapons. This strategic posture implies that an 'offensive' use would be immoral, but presupposes that there is conceivably some judicious, responsible way to employ nuclear weapons defensively, presumably only in response to the most extreme dangers and after a painstaking selection of strictly military targets. But it is almost inconceivable that, in the employment of the nuclear missiles actually in our stockpiles, there could be any specific focus on military targets.

Because of the tremendous firepower involved, the genetic and ecological consequences of radiation, the possibility of giving rise to a 'nuclear winter', and the probability of escalation, any use of nuclear weapons now seems necessarily to entail destructive and lethal consequences reaching far beyond the neutralisation of any 'enemy installation' at which it is directed. There is a very real and sobering analogy to be drawn between the use (even defensive) of nuclear weaponry and the smaller scale 'terrorist' attacks which are viewed by most people now with moral outrage. For both terrorism and nuclear warfare make no effective distinction between military and civilian, combatant and noncombatant, guilty and innocent. The indiscriminate, 'terroristic' aspect of nuclear weaponry places them in a *sui generis* category. Even one who believes in the possibility of a just, defensive war must balk when it comes to supporting measures which must necessarily cause indiscriminate destruction on a monstrous scale. Can any end justify the use of these means? Is any threat sufficient to justify the use of indiscriminate killing as a countermeasure? Nuclear weapons are commonly categorised as just one more element in our national defence arsenal. But if there is the possibility of morally justified killing with the other weapons in our defence arsenal, there seems to be no such possibility with nuclear weapons. They would seem to be not just another weapon, but an intrinsically immoral device to use, to threaten to use, or even to possess. Those who concentrate on the political and military problems connected with the possession and deployment of nuclear weapons are making a category mistake. Their attention should be squarely focused on the much more relevant moral question as to whether the extermination of almost the entire world, in a futile attempt to save our own nation or allies from extermination, should even enter into our mind as an option to consider.

## 6(c) 3.3. *Combating Overpopulation*

It is almost taken as a truism now that mankind has a moral obligation to reduce population to prevent economic and ecological crises of global proportions. But the facts seem to indicate otherwise: in the world today there are approximately 5,000,000,000 people. If we were to take all these people and put them into the North American state of Texas (whose area is approximately 7,450,000,000,000 square feet), each individual would have a little over 1400 square feet of horizontal living space. (Subtractions would have to be made because of considerations of habitability, but compensating additions would also be made because of the possibility of adding 'vertical' space through multi-storey buildings, etc.) Statistics like this merely indicate that the problem of overpopulation should not be oversimplified as a problem of too little living *space*. The problem of overpopulation seems rather to be a political problem, which bifurcates in two directions:

(a) *Urban congestion* Movements around the world away from the land and into the cities create pockets of overpopulation. The central urban areas in many countries become overridden with poverty, crime and various social problems, leading many of the sufficiently affluent to move out to the suburbs; layers of suburbs eventually surround the city, while urban blight and social alienation in the central city grow to sometimes explosive proportions. In other cities and countries, concentric layers of slums gradually expand outward around a more affluent central urban population. In either scenario, the concentric population expansion outward from the city centre tends eventually to constrict and choke that centre. Some urbanologists (for example, Gottoman and Doxiadis), resigned to the irreversibility of the movement to the city, have suggested plans for longitudinal, rather than concentric, expansion of the city (Doxiadis suggests as reasonable a maximum world-wide urban population of 33,000,000,000 people), which would help to obviate the explosive syndrome we are most familiar with. Such plans exemplify political approaches which, if implemented, could mitigate those aspects of overpopulation connected with 'the urban problem'.

(b) *Poverty* Karl Marx, in his frequent criticisms of the Malthusian theory concerning the relation of food supply to population, observed that the overpopulation 'problem' in capitalistic systems is tied in with the necessity of building up a huge industrial 'reserve army' of labourers with the skills or availability desired by potential employers.[17] According to Friedrich Engels, our concept of 'overpopulation' in general is connected with poverty: we do not speak of relatively well-off concentrations of people as 'overpopulated'.[18] Others besides Marxists have noted the connection of overpopulation with unemployment and poverty rather than with pure and simple demographic density of population.[19]

It is quite possible that the problems of overpopulation connected with urban congestion and poverty can be solved (as well as one can expect human problems to be solved) within present capitalistic structures; while historical precedents might lead us to doubt that the radical Marxist solution would be any more effective. Some have even suggested that increases of population, far from being threatening, are salutary developments, which will help bring about structural ameliorations and redistribution of wealth.[20]

Whether or not such a sanguine attitude towards population increases is warranted, an important step in intellectual clarity could be made if it were more widely realised that it is a category mistake to maintain that 'overpopulation' is a problem which we have a moral obligation to combat by education, birth control, etc. Rather, it is a political–economic problem, a particularly aggravated form of some perennial complications associated especially with urbanisation and industrialisation.[21] There may be a moral obligation to change political structures giving rise to 'overpopulation' (based on the aforementioned subjunction of politics to morality) but there is not any moral obligation to work directly for the reduction of population.

## 6(d)   MORALITY AND LEGALITY

### 6(d) 1.   Divergences

Some have suggested that in a democratic society even private practices (for example, homosexual practices between consenting adults) can be subjected to public laws, if there is among the majority a strong repugnance for, and a strong consensus about the immorality of, these practices.[22] However, it would seem necessary that some serious public threat be demonstrably associated with the 'private immorality', and also that the majority also are willing to pay higher taxes if these should be necessary to cover expenses connected with the increase in personnel, equipment, etc., required for enforcement of the laws. For example, for the prohibition of certain homosexual practices, there would have to be massive moral disapproval and repugnance, along with a serious threat such as rampant juvenile prostitution or an epidemic of AIDS or some other deadly disease which was shown to be clearly associated with such practices, and also a public willingness to accept an increase in property or income taxes to augment enforcement potential – a combination of factors that it is hardly possible to imagine. (The question of whether the majority is actually *correct* in its moral consensus is a peripheral question, from the purely legislative viewpoint.)

In a pluralistic, democratic society the proper and undisputed province of the police is, in addition to enforcement of civil laws (for example, traffic laws), the enforcement of restrictions against those types of public morality (for example, murder, theft, rape) which clearly pose a threat to the public safety or welfare. When an action which is perceived as public immorality, for example, philandering by public officials is not also perceived as a public threat, it will not ordinarily be subject to legal sanctions. Thus the legal diverges from the moral in being concerned primarily only with a certain subcategory of public morality, as well as extra-moral civil matters.

## 6(d) 2. Subjunctions

### 6(d) 2.1. *The Subjunction of Legality to Morality*
The most important area where the legal is subjoined to the moral in Western law courts is in the concept of *mens rea* ('guilty intention'). Some crimes are tried according to 'strict liability' (responsibility for the act, no matter what the intention or what the circumstances); but for a great number of crimes conviction is not possible unless it be shown that there was definitely a subjective unethical intent on the part of the criminal. Psychological compulsions (for example, kleptomania) and states of insanity (for example, paranoic delusions) are considered valid extenuating factors in our courts. The requirement for proving *mens rea* causes endless difficulties and complexity, and is often abused by defence lawyers; but it also testifies to the recognition of the importance of 'subjective' moral intentions in the public moral judgements made in a democratic society.

Another area in which legality is subjoined to morality is in the concept of 'equity', which allows the courts to use very general ethical principles in judging cases where no specific law or precedent seems to apply. Formerly in England and the US there were special courts designated as courts of equity. But now the concept is applied in regular courts when situations arise in which its use is called for.

### 6(d) 2.2. *The Subjunction of Morality to Legality*
It seems that the laws can in some cases have an educative moral influence on a society. For example, the laws against bribery in

Western democratic countries, the laws against duelling that were eventually enforced in nineteenth-century Germany, the rather strict laws against income tax fraud in the United States (as compared with other countries) – have been effective not only in eliminating immoral practices, but also possibly in eliminating the tendencies and intents to engage in such practices. The laws which were eventually passed against the burning of witches, and slavery, and various forms of racial and sexual discrimination have also no doubt gradually produced a wholesale betterment in the moral attitude of vast populations. The most controversial use of the 'educative' aspect of laws is the enactment by legislators of laws which they themselves favour morally, but which may not be favoured by a majority of their constituents. If, for example, 'pro-life' legislators enacted laws against abortion when there was not a clear consensus for such laws among those they represent, there would be an apparent conflict between what the legislators felt to be their moral duty, and their duty to represent the desires of their constituents. If, on the other hand, a representative must *always* act in accord with the desires of his or her constituents, she or he might be best replaced by a computerised system which could simply and accurately register and implement the desires of the constituents in question. If we prefer the expertise of a person over the automation of a computer, we must perhaps show some deference to the moral judgement of legislators at least in cases where there is no strong and overwhelming majority pro or con.

## 6(d) 3.   A Category Mistake: the Prohibition of Abortion

Some Catholic theologians, priests, and nuns, and a few Catholics in public life, such as Geraldine Ferraro and Governor Cuomo of New York in the 1984 US presidential campaign, have issued a type of statement which seems, at first sight, to be inconsistent. They have asserted that they are personally opposed to abortion, but do not believe their personal views should be incorporated in the laws. Those who accuse them of inconsistency, however, are making a category mistake, if they believe that personal moral convictions must necessarily be translated into a conviction concerning laws and enforcement. As was argued above (section d[1]), legality clearly diverges from morality by requiring a serious public threat and concerted public support for something to be declared illegal. Abortion, however, does not pose any serious public threat (the unborn foetuses themselves are not at present understood to be members of 'the public'), but, on the contrary, the prohibition of abortion would probably constitute such a threat (if one takes into account the probable emergence of underground 'abortion mills' and the health and safety hazards involved); and likewise, there seems to be a lack of the serious public financial support which would be required if anti-abortion laws were implemented (requiring tax increases for expansion of the police force, for child support, for public care of unwanted children, etc.). Those who maintain that moral opposition to abortion must be consistently translated into legal sanctions often argue that abortion is murder and should be outlawed like any form of murder. But abortion, *unless and until* the foetus is given public recognition as a person, is 'private' murder (for want of a better description). That is, abortion is not murder in a public and legal sense, since the foetus, at least prior to the final stages of gestation, is not generally recognised as a *legal* person with all the rights accruing to citizenship. If the foetus were to be not just morally but legally recognised as a person, by legislation or a constitutional amendment, the support for such a recognition would indicate that the definition of the 'public' and hence of the 'public threat' had clearly changed, and presumably also that there was now a sufficient public willingness to support the enforcement of laws against this public threat, financially and otherwise. But until that point is reached, the outlawing of abortion in a pluralistic, democratic society, on the basis of moral beliefs, and without a significant consensus, would be an example of a legal–moral category mistake.

# Conclusion

As we survey the history of moral theory in Western philosophy, we find what seems at first to be a *melange* of conflicting and even contradictory ideas about the morally good. But one central area of unanimous concern does seem to emerge from our consideration: the concern with what is distinctively appropriate to *human nature*, which can be interpreted hedonistically or altruistically, empirically or *a priori*, individualistically or with an emphasis on social or cosmic solidarity. Moral theories can even give us an index to the philosophical or non-philosophical anthropology in which they are rooted, so that, if we were in doubt about our anthropological stance, our preference in moral theory can help to clear up these doubts. While it would be over-optimistic to hope to settle the long-standing disputes among moral theorists, it is within our grasp to refine our own concepts of humanity and the specific 'good' congruent to humanity, possibly by searching out a middle-of-the-road, correlativistic position between what seem to be the most extreme points of view, including extreme subjectivism and extreme objectivism. The more nuanced points of view that we finally etch out for ourselves will not necessarily give us a fail-safe key for solving practical moral issues and dilemmas, but will help us to disentangle the moral considerations from other competing considerations with respect to contemporary moral controversies in our milieu, as well as with respect to our personal decision-making.

# Notes

## Notes to the Preface

1. D. D. Raphael, *Moral Philosophy* (Oxford University Press, 1981) p. 9.
2. G. W. F. Hegel, *Logic*, trs. W. Wallace (Oxford University Press, 1931) § 41, remarks.
3. Some confusion attends the use of these terms. Practical judgements about issues such as euthanasia and abortion are often given as examples of doing 'normative ethics'. But surely such judgements are more precisely endeavours in 'practical' ethics, on which normative ethical theories (for example, utilitarianism) may have an influence. Utilitarianism, the Kantian criterion of universalisability, natural law, etc., are generally considered 'normative' ethical theories, but they surely presuppose some meta-ethical positions regarding the meaning of 'good', 'right', etc. In the twentieth century there has been a tendency to eschew normative ethics for meta-ethics, thought by many to be the only genuine *philosophical* ethics. But as Roger Hancock shows in *Twentieth-Century Ethics* (New York and London: Columbia University Press, 1974) pp. 3–11, 188–97, it is almost as impossible to develop meta-ethical theories which have no normative implications, as it is to propound normative ethical theories without meta-ethical presuppositions. Many mainstream analytic ethicians may be attempting the impossible.

## Notes to Chapter 1: Aristotelian 'Happiness', Revisited

1. Aristotle, *Nicomachean Ethics*, I, 7, 1098a, 1099b, 1101a.
2. Søren Kierkegaard, *The Concept of Dread*, trs. Walter Lowrie (Princeton, N.J.: Princeton University Press, 1957) p. 15.
3. Aristotle, *Nicomachean Ethics*, I, 10, 1100b, 33–1101a, 8.
4. *Ibid.*, I, 8, 1099a, 17; VIII, 6, 1158a, 24–5. For an extensive treatment of the Aristotelian idea of *eudaimonia*, and its relationship to virtue, subjective happiness and aesthetics, see Elizabeth Telfer, *Happiness* (New York: St Martin's Press, 1980) esp. chs 2 and 3.
5. Plato, *Euthyphro*, 157A, B.
6. Immanuel Kant, *Fundamental Principles of the Metaphysic of Morals*, trs. Thomas K. Abbott (New York: Bobbs-Merrill, 1949) pp. 16–17.
7. *Ibid.*, pp. 77, 28n, 19.
8. *Ibid.*, p. 59; and Immanuel Kant, *Critique of Practical Reason*, trs. L. W. Beck (New York: Bobbs-Merrill, 1956) pp. 119–23.

## Notes to Chapter 2: Aesthetic Good

1. Arthur K. Bierman, *The Philosophy of Urban Existence* (Athens, Ohio: Ohio University Press, 1973) ch. IV.
2. See, for example, Edward Bullough, '"Psychical Distance" as a Factor in Art and an Aesthetic Principle', in *Aesthetics and the Philosophy of Criticism*, ed. M. Levich (New York: Random House, 1963).
3. See, for example, D. H. Parker, *The Principles of Aesthetics* (New York: Appleton-Century-Crofts, 1946; and London: Greenwood Press, 1977) p. 48; and M. Dessoir, *Aesthetics and Theory of Art* (Detroit, Mich.: Wayne State University Press, 1970) pp. 71–3.
4. Monroe Beardsley, *Aesthetics: Problems in the Philosophy of Criticism* (New York: Harcourt, Brace, 1958).
5. Frederick Kainz, *Aesthetics: The Science*, trs. H. Schueller (Detroit, Mich.: Wayne State University Press, 1962) p. 252.
6. R. Rorty, *Philosophy and the Mirror of Nature* (Oxford: Basil Blackwell, 1980) pp. 336ff. Rorty's attempt at clarification contrasts remarkably with Paul Ramsey's argument in *The Truth of Value* (Atlantic Highlands, N.J.: Humanities Press, 1985) chs 7–8, that the words 'subjective' and 'objective' are so hopelessly ambiguous that we should 'sweep them away' (*ibid.*, p. 79). But possibly some explicit efforts to control the recalcitrant terms should precede the Herculean task of obliteration.
7. Howard Kainz, *Ethica Dialectica* (The Hague: Nijhoff, 1979) p. 50.
8. See the commentaries of Aquinas on Aristotle, *De Anima*, II, 6, 418a, 20 and *Nicomachean Ethics*, VI, 11, 1143a, 35ff. For a thorough and erudite exposition of the *vis cogitativa*, see George Klubertanz, *The Discursive Power* (St Louis, Mo.: Modern Schoolman, 1952).
9. Thomas Aquinas, in *VI Ethicorum Aristotelis*, Lect. IX (with reference to Aristotle, *Nicomachean Ethics*, VI, 11).
10. Thomas Aquinas, *Summa theologiae*, I–2, q. 74, a. 3, ad 1.
11. Johann Gottlieb Fichte, *The Science [sic] of Ethics*, trs. Kroeger (London: Kegan Paul, 1907) p. 179 (German title: *Das System der Sittenlehre*).
12. A recent example is Stuart Hampshire's *Morality and Conflict* (Cambridge, Mass.: Harvard University Press and Oxford: Blackwell, 1983) ch. 5. Classical intuitionism is exemplified in W. D. Ross, *The Foundations of Ethics* (Oxford: Clarenden Press, 1939); Richard Price, *A Review of the Principal Questions in Morals* (Oxford: Clarendon Press, 1948); and E. F. Caritt, *The Theory of Morals* (London: Oxford University Press, 1928).
13. William H. Sheldon, *The Varieties of Temperament* (New York: Harper and Row, 1942) p. 4.
14. Gordon Allport, *Pattern and Growth in Personality* (New York: Holt, Rinehart and Winston, 1961) p. 34.
15. For example, Aristotle, *Nicomachean Ethics*, VII, 7; III, 8; IV, 5. Concerning the extensive influence of Hippocratean theories on Aristotle's ethics, see Theodore Tracy, *Physiological Theory and the Doctrine of the Mean in Plato and Aristotle* (Paris: Mouton, 1969) pp. 222ff.
16. See, for example, Immanuel Kant, *Anthropology*, trs. M. Gregor (The Hague: Nijhoff, 1974); and G. W. F. Hegel, 'Anthropology' in his

*Philosophy of Mind*, trs. W. Wallace (Oxford: Clarendon Press, 1971) § 395.

17. H. J. Eysenck, *The Biological Basis of Personality* (Springfield, Ill.: Charles C. Thomas, 1967) pp. 34–7. Jung's major work on the subject is *Psychological Types, or The Psychology of Individuation*, trs. H. Godwin Baynes (London: Routledge and Kegan Paul, 1923).

18. See, for example, Erwin O. Strassman, 'Physique, Temperament, and Intelligence in Infertile Women', *International Journal of Fertility*, vol. 9 (1964) no. 2, pp. 297–314.

19. Eysenck, *Biological Basis of Personality*, p. 37.

20. *Ibid.*, p. 112.

21. H. J. Eysenck, *Sex and Personality* (Austin, Tx.: University of Texas Press, and West Compton House: Shepton Mallet, Som., 1976) pp. 12–13; see also pp. 197–8.

22. Cynthia C. Bisbee, Robert W. Mullaly and Humphry Osmond, 'Temperament and Psychiatric Illness', *Journal of Orthomolecular Psychiatry* vol. 12 (1983) no. 1, pp. 19–25.

23. Eysenck, *Biological Basis of Personality*, pp. 38–40.

24. *Ibid.*, p. 41.

25. Lee Willerman, *The Psychology of Individual and Group Differences* (San Francisco, Cal. and Oxford: W. H. Freeman, 1979) p. 207.

26. See, for example, David Lester, 'Deviation in Sheldonian Physique-Temperament Match and Neuroticism', *Psychological Reports*, vol. 4 (Dec. 1977) no. 3, pt 1, p. 942; and James Q. Wilson and Richard J. Herrnstein, *Crime and Human Nature* (New York: Simon and Schuster, 1985) pp. 81–90.

27. See Willerman, *The Psychology of Individual and Group Differences*, p. 203. See also Horace Stewart, 'Body Type, Personality, Temperament, and Psychotherapeutic Treatment of Female Adolescents', *Adolescence*, vol. 17 (Fall, 1982) pp. 621–5; Horace Stewart, 'Body Type, Personality, Temperament, and Psychotherapeutic Treatment of Male Adolescents', in *Adolescence*, vol. 15 (Winter 1980) pp. 927–32; Eysenck, *Sex and Personality*, pp. 197–8; Arnold Gesell and Frances Ilg, *The Child from Five to Ten* (New York and London: Harper, 1946); and Wilson and Herrnstein, *Crime and Human Nature*, pp. 81ff.

28. Sheldon, *The Varieties of Temperament*, p. 91.

29. *Ibid.*, pp. 39, 41. 47.

30. *Ibid.*, pp. 59, 64.

31. *Ibid.*, p. 14.

32. Eysenck, *Sex and Personality*, p. 219; Wilson and Herrnstein (*Crime and Human Nature*) note that crime is 'predominantly male behavior'.

33. See, for example, Carol Tavris and Carole Offir, *The Longest War: Sex Differences in Perspective* (New York: Harcourt Brace Jovanovich, 1977) p. 54f. This book draws heavily on, and supplements, the earlier work of Eleanor Macoby and Carol Jacklin in *The Psychology of Sex Differences* (Stanford, Cal.: Stanford University Press, 1974).

34. Tavris and Offir, *The Longest War*, p. 94.

35. *Ibid.*, pp. 35–7.

36. See, for example, William G. Sumner, *Folkways* (New York: Ginn, 1907)

and Ruth Benedict, 'Anthropology and the Abnormal', in *The Philosophy of Society*, ed. R. Beehle (London: Methuen, 1978); cf. also F. H. Bradley, 'My Station and Its Duties', in his *Ethical Studies* (Oxford: Clarendon Press, 1927).

37. Henry Sidgwick, *The Methods of Ethics*, 7th rev. edn (Chicago, Ill.: University of Chicago Press, 1901) p. 246.
38. See, for example, Edward O. Wilson, *Sociobiology: The New Synthesis* (Cambridge, Mass.: Harvard University Press, 1975) and, by the same author, *On Human Nature* (Cambridge, Mass.: Harvard University Press, 1978).
39. Peter Singer, *The Expanding Circle: Ethics and Sociobiology* (New York: Farrer, Straus & Giroux, and Oxford: Oxford University Press, 1981) pp. 13–14.
40. For a critique of sociobiology, see *ibid.*, chs 4–6; Marshall Sahlin, *The Use and Abuse of Biology* (Ann Arbor, Mich.: University of Michigan Press, 1976); and Peter Singer, 'Ethics and Sociobiology', *Philosophy and Public Affairs*, vol. I (Winter 1982) no. 1, pp. 40–64.
41. Peter Singer, *The Expanding Circle*, pp. 16, 18, 37ff.
42. Lawrence Kohlberg, 'Education for Justice', in *Moral Education*, ed. T. Sizer (Cambridge, Mass.: Harvard University Press, 1970) pp. 57–83.
43. *Ibid.*, pp. 71–2.
44. See Carol Gilligan, *In a Different Voice: Psychological Theory and Women's Development* (Cambridge, Mass. and London: Harvard University Press, 1982) and 'Woman's Place in Man's Life Cycle', *Harvard Educational Review*, vol. 49 (1979) pp. 431–41. See also J. M. Murphy and Carol Gilligan, 'Moral Development in Late Adolescence and Adulthood: a Critique and Reconstruction of Kohlberg's Theory', *Human Development*, vol. 23 (1980) pp. 77–104. Nel Nodding, *Caring: A Feminine Approach to Ethics and Moral Education* (Berkeley and Los Angeles, Cal.: University of California Press, 1984) offers some good examples of the implications of Gilligan's theory in normative ethics.
45. See Lawrence Kohlberg, C. Levine and A. Hewer, *Moral Stages: A Current Formulation and a Response to Critics* (New York: S. Korger, 1983) pp. 121ff. See also Owen J. Flanagan, Jr, 'Virtue, Sex and Gender: Some Philosophical Reflections on the Moral Psychology Debate', *Ethics*, vol. 92 (April 1982) pp. 499–512; and Annette C. Baier, 'What Do Women Want in a Moral Theory?', *Nous*, vol. 19 (1985) no. 1, pp. 53–64. Baier, in 'Hume, the Women's Theorist?', in *Women and Moral Theory*, Kittag and Meyers (eds) (Totowa, N.J.: Rowman and Allanfield, 1987), shows how the characteristics which Gilligan discerns in female moral attitudes are also key features in Hume's moral theory: an 'aesthetic/moral' approach, strongly influenced by 'moral sense' theories.
46. See, for example, Carolyn Edwards, 'Moral Development in Comparative Cultural Perspectives', in *Cultural Perspectives on Child Development*, eds D. Wagner and H. Stevenson (New York: Freeman, 1982); Carolyn Edwards, 'The Comparative Study of the Development of Moral Judgment and Reasoning', in *Handbook of Cross-Cultural Human Development*, ed. R. Munroe (New York: Garland, 1981); Lawrence

Kohlberg, *The Psychology of Moral Development* (San Francisco, Cal.: Harper and Row, 1984) pp. 582–620; and Kohlberg, Levine and Hewer, *Moral Stages*, pp. 109–115.

## Notes to Chapter 3: Moral Good

1. Mary Midgley, 'Is "Moral" a Dirty Word?', *Philosophy*, vol. XLVII (July 1972) no. 181, pp. 210ff.
2. *Ibid.*, p. 215.
3. David Gauthier, 'On the Refutation of Utilitarianism', in *The Limits of Utilitarianism*, ed. Harlan B. Miller and William H. Williamson (Minneapolis, Minn.: University of Minnesota Press, 1982) p. 151.
4. John Dewey, *Human Nature and Conduct* (New York: Random House, 1930) p. 326.
5. Kurt Baier, *The Moral Point of View* (Ithaca, New York: Cornell University Press, 1958) pp. 188ff.
6. Hampshire, *Morality and Conflict*, ch. 5.
7. Henry Veatch, 'Are there Non-Moral Goods?', *The New Scholasticism*, vol. LII (Autumn 1978) no. 4, p. 476.
8. Dewey, *Human Nature and Conduct*, p. 44.
9. Alasdair MacIntyre, *After Virtue: A Study in Moral Theory* (Notre Dame, Ind.: Notre Dame University Press, and London: Duckworth, 1981) p. 194.
10. *Ibid.*, pp. 195–6.
11. Kant, *Fundamental Principles of the Metaphysic of Morals*, p. 15.
12. John Dewey, *Theory of the Moral Life* (New York: Holt, Rinehart and Winston, 1960) pp. 110, 90.
13. H. Kainz, *The Philosophy of Man: A New Introduction to some Perennial Issues* (Tuscaloosa, Ala.: University of Alabama Press, 1980) ch. 1.
14. Singer, *The Expanding Circle*, pp. 113, 116, 117.
15. Plato, *The Republic*, trs. B. Jowett (New York: Random House, 1937) II, 360A.
16. See especially Book IX of *The Republic*.
17. Kant, *Fundamental Principles of the Metaphysic of Morals*, pp. 14–15.
18. *Ibid.*
19. *Ibid.*
20. *Ibid.*, p. 19n; see also p.59n.
21. Quoted by John Dewey in his *Ethics* (New York: Holt, 1908) p. 349.
22. Jean-Paul Sartre, *Being and Nothingness*, trs. H. Barnes (New York: Washington Square Press, 1966) p. 767; and 'Existentialism is a Humanism' in *Existentialism*, ed. Walter Kaufmann (New York: Meridian, 1956) p. 307.
23. Sartre, *Being and Nothingness*, pp. 17ff.
24. *Ibid.*, pp. 66ff.
25. *Ibid.*, p. 65.
26. *Ibid.*, p. 70.

27. Quoted in Singer, *The Expanding Circle*, p. 136, except for Buddhism (see Udana-Varga, 5, 18).
28. Aristotle, *Nicomachean Ethics*, IX, 8, 1168b–1169a, and II, 6, 1107a.
29. Richard Norman, *The Moral Philosophers* (Oxford: Clarendon Press, 1983) p. 184.
30. A. E. Taylor, *Aristotle* (New York: Dover, 1955) p. 95. See also Theodore Tracy, *Physiological Theory and the Doctrine of the Mean in Plato and Aristotle*, pp. 222ff.
31. Aristotle, *Nicomachean Ethics*, II, 9, 1109b.
32. *Ibid.*, I, 8.
33. Hampshire, *Morality and Conflict*, pp. 101ff.
34. Aristotle, *Nicomachean Ethics*, x, 9.
35. Benedict Spinoza, *Ethics*, trs. W. H. White and A. H. Stirling (Oxford: Oxford University Press, 1927) v, Prop. 3.
36. *Ibid.*, Prop. 4.
37. Sigmund Freud, *The Ego and the Id*, trs. Joan Riviere (New York: Norton, 1960) pp. 30ff.
38. Spinoza, *Ethics*, IV, Prop. 20ff.
39. Sigmund Freud, *Civilization and Its Discontents*, trs. James Strachey (New York: Norton, 1961; London: Hogarth, 1963) ch. 5 and *passim*.
40. See Spinoza, *Ethics*, v, Prop. 30ff.
41. Freud, *The Ego and the Id*, p. 15.
42. Spinoza, *Ethics*, III, Prop. 2, note.
43. *Ibid.*, v, Prop. 4.
44. *Ibid.*, v, Prop. 10.
45. *Ibid.*, v, Prop. 10; and IV, Prop. 46.
46. Adam Smith, *The Theory of Moral Sentiments* (Oxford: Clarendon Press, 1976) pp. 115 and 118.
47. Kant, *Fundamental Principles of the Metaphysic of Morals*, p. 38.
48. *Ibid.*, p. 41.
49. *Ibid.*, p. 47n.
50. *Ibid.*
51. *Ibid.*
52. See Henry Veatch, 'The Rational Justification of Moral Principles: Can There Be Such a Thing?', *Review of Metaphysics*, vol. XXXI, (Dec. 1977) no. 2, pp. 218–19.
53. See Immanuel Kant, 'On the Supposed Right to Tell Lies from Benevolent Motives', in *The Critique of Practical Reason and Other Works on the Theory of Ethics* (London: Longman, Green, 1909) p. 362.
54. Marcus Singer, 'The Categorical Imperative', *Philosophical Review*, vol. LXIII (Oct. 1954) no. 4, pp. 577–91.
55. Julius Ebbinghaus, 'Interpretation and Misinterpretation of the Categorical Imperative', *Philosophical Quarterly*, vol. IV (April 1954) no. 15, pp. 97–108.
56. Kant, *Fundamental Principles of the Metaphysic of Morals*, pp. 45–6.
57. *Ibid.*, pp. 46 and 64.
58. Raphael, *Moral Philosophy*, p. 58.
59. Kant, *Fundamental Principles of the Metaphysic of Morals*, p. 46.
60. *Ibid.*, p. 47.

61. MacIntyre, *After Virtue*, p. 105. Richard Taylor, in *Ethics, Faith and Reason* (Englewood Cliffs, N.J.: Prentice-Hall, 1981), ch. 14 and *passim*, goes even further, portraying modern ethics in general as a 'ghost' of the 'divine laws' of religion.

62. For a discussion of the implications of this research, see H. Kainz, *The Philosophy of Man*, ch. 1.

63. *Ibid.*, pp. 14f.

64. Plato, *Phaedo*, 96A–100A.

65. Plato, *Apology*, 38A.

66. Epictetus, *Discourses*, II, 1, 32.

67. Søren Kierkegaard, *Either/Or*, trs. Walter Lowrie (New York: Anchor, 1959) II, p. 327.

68. *Ibid.*, p. 263.

69. *Ibid.*, pp. 255–6.

70. On the difficulties connected with Kierkegaard's account of transcendence, see my 'Kierkegaard's "Three Stages" and the Levels of Spiritual Maturity', *Modern Schoolman*, vol. LII (May 1975) no. 4, pp. 368f.

71. Kierkegaard, *Either/Or*, II, pp. 171, 181, 275, 296.

72. *Ibid.*, pp. 46, 62, 91–6, 309.

73. Kant, *Fundamental Principles of the Metaphysic of Morals*, p. 55 (italics added).

74. p. 31 above.

75. p. 60 above.

76. See, for example, Michael Grant, *Jesus: An Historian's Review of the Gospels* (New York: Charles Scribner's Sons, 1977; London: Sphere, 1978) ch. 1.

77. H. J. Paton, *The Categorical Imperative* (London: Hutchinson, 1967) pp. 187f.

78. Kant, *The Critique of Pure Reason*, p. 637 (A 808 = B 836).

79. See in the Bible Romans 12: 4–5; I Corinthians 12; Colossians 1: 15–18, 2: 6–10; Ephesians 4: 11–16.

80. Kant, *Fundamental Principles of the Metaphysic of Morals*, pp. 56f.

81. See Immanuel Kant, 'The Idea for a Universal History from a Cosmopolitan Point of View' and 'Perpetual Peace', in *Kant on History*, ed. and trs. F. W. Beck (Indianapolis, Ind.: Bobbs-Merrill, 1963) especially pp. 18f. and 124ff.

82. See p. 36 above.

83. See Erik Wolf, *Das Problem der Naturrechtslehre, Versuch einer Orientierung* (Karlsruhe; Müller, 1955) ch. 1; and Ernst Bloch, *Natural Law and Human Dignity*, trs. D. Schmidt (Cambridge, Mass. and London: MIT Press, 1986) pp. 192–3.

84. Cicero, *De Republica*, III, 22; cited in R. Wilkin, T. Davitt and A. Harding, *Origins of the Natural Law Tradition* (Port Washington, N.Y.: Kennikat Press, 1971).

85. Marcus Aurelius, *Meditations*, VII, 55.

86. Epictetus, *The Golden Sayings*, xv–xvi.

87. See p. 7 above.

88. See Aristotle, *Rhetoric* I, chs 13 and 15; *Nicomachean Ethics* v, 7, 1134b,

18ff.; Thomas Aquinas, *Commentary on the 'Nicomachean Ethics'*, trs. C. I. Litzigner (Chicago, Ill.: Regnery, 1964) I, pp. 441–2, 468. See also Patrick Farrell, 'Sources of St Thomas' Concept of Natural Law', *The Thomist*, vol. xx (July 1957) no. 3, pp. 249–54; and W. von Leyden, *Aristotle on Equality and Justice* (N.Y.: St Martin's Press, 1985) pp. 71–90.

89. Aquinas, *Summa theologiae*, I–2, q. 91, a. 2.

90. *Ibid.*

91. *Ibid.*, q. 94, a. 2.

92. *Ibid.*, q. 94, a. 4; and Supplement, 9.65, a. 1, ad 8um.

93. *Ibid.*, II–2, q. 154, a. 12.

94. Aristotle, *Politics*, I, 5.

95. See, for example, Aquinas, *Summa theologiae*, II–2, q. 10, a. 10.

96. Cf., for example, the papal Bull, *Romanus Pontifex*, of Pope Nicholas V (1454) and, in more recent times, the Instruction of the Holy Office on 20 June 1866, which concludes: 'It is not contrary to the natural and divine law for a slave to be sold, exchanged or given.' This position was finally reversed in Pope Leo XIII's encyclical *Rerum Novarum* (1891), which declares slavery unjustifiable.

97. Aquinas, *Summa theologiae*, II–1, q. 94, a. 4; II–2, q. 57, a. 3, ad. 2.

98. Hugo Grotius, *The Law of War and Peace*, trs. L. Loomis (Roslyn, New York: Walter Black, 1949) I, 1.

99. Jeremy Bentham, *An Introduction to the Principles of Morals and Legislation*, ed. J. H. Burns, James Henderson and H. L. A. Hart (New York: Russell and Russell, and Atheon Press, 1962) ch. I; ch. II, xiv.

100. Garry Wills, *Inventing America: Jefferson's Declaration of Independence* (New York: Doubleday, 1978; and London: Athlone, 1980) pp. 150–3.

101. *Ibid.*, p. 149. On Beccaria's similar orientation, see *ibid.*, p. 153.

102. See xiii, 24 above.

103. See pp. xiii above.

104. See the Preface, p. xiv.

105. See p. 36 above.

106. Quoted in Maximilien Rubel and Margaret Manale, *Marx Without Myth* (New York: Harper, 1976) p. 330. This characterisation of Marx is more fully developed by Engels in his *Socialism: Utopian and Scientific*, section II.

107. Karl Marx, *Capital*, trs. B. Fowkes (New York: Vintage, 1977) I, Preface, and ch. 24: 5.

108. Karl Marx and Friedrich Engels, *The Communist Manifesto*, trs. F. Randall (New York: Washington Square Press, 1964) pp. 90–1.

109. See, for example, Karl Marx, 'The German Ideology', in *The Marx–Engels Reader*, ed. David McLellan (Oxford: Oxford University Press, 1977) p. 183.

110. On this issue, see Richard Miller, *Analyzing Marx: Morality, Power and History* (Princeton, N.J.: Princeton University Press, 1984) ch. 1; Sidney Hook, *From Hegel to Marx* (Ann Arbor, Mich.: University of Michigan Press, 1962) pp. 51–2; John McMurtry, *The Structure of Marx's World-View* (Princeton, N.J.: Princeton University Press, 1978) pp. 238–9; Steven Lukes, *Marxism and Morality* (Oxford: Clarendon Press, 1985) p. 58; and Charles Wei-Hsun Fu, 'Marxism–Leninism–

Maoism as an Ethical Theory', *Journal of Chinese Philosophy*, vol. 5 (1978) pp. 343–62. Robert Tucker, in his *Philosophy and Myth in Karl Marx* (Cambridge: Cambridge University Press, 1965) pp. 16–18, distances himself from the positions of Sidney Hook, Karl Popper, Herbert Marcuse and others (one might add John McMurtry to his list), all of whom hold that Marx was an ethicist. Tucker maintains that Marx is a moralist, not a moral philosopher. But he defines 'moral philosophy' (*ibid.*, p. 15) as an 'inquiry into the nature of the supreme good for man or the criterion of right conduct'. But this is a definition most germane to twentieth-century Anglo-American ethics, which is largely equated with meta-ethics, is sharply differentiated from political and economic philosophy, and is extremely self-conscious about the meaning of 'good' and 'right'.

111. Rubel and Manale, *Marx without Myth*, p. 191.
112. See Marx, *Capital*, trs. B. Fowkes (New York: Random House, 1977) pp. 92, 459, 493n. On the Marx–Darwin relationship, see Paul Heyer, *Nature, Human Nature, and Society* (Westport, Conn.: Greenwood Press, 1982) pp. 47–9, 54–7, 65–8; and Bruce Mazlich, *The Meaning of Karl Marx* (Oxford: Oxford University Press, 1984) pp. 17, 132, 160n, 168n.
113. See above, pp. 78–9.
114. Karl Marx, 'A Contribution to the Critique of Hegel's Philosophy of Right', in Karl Marx, *Critique of Hegel's Philosophy of Right*, trs. J. O'Malley (Cambridge: Cambridge University Press, 1970) pp. 141–2.
115. See, for example, Karl Marx, *The Economic and Philosophic Manuscripts of 1844*, trs. Martin Milligan (New York: International Publishers, 1964) pp. 144, 155.
116. A concept of nature which is incompatible with the theory of evolution would be outdated. On evolutionary ethics as a possible extension of natural law ethics, see John Deely and Raymond Nogar, *The Problem of Evolution: A Study of the Philosophical Repercussions of Evolutionary Science* (New York: Appleton-Century-Crofts, 1973) pp. 187, 197, 207n. It goes without saying that only a non-Darwinian, teleological interpretation of evolution could give support to natural law theory.
117. See G. W. F. Hegel, *The Philosophy of Right*, trs. T. M. Knox (Oxford: Oxford University Press, 1967) §§ 129–41; and H. Kainz, *Hegel's Philosophy of Right, with Marx's Commentary: A Handbook for Students* (The Hague: Nijhoff, 1974) pp. 22–4.
118. Friedrich Nietzsche, *The Will to Power*, trs. W. Kaufmann (New York: Vintage, 1968) especially the section entitled 'Anti-Darwin'.
119. There is some dispute as to whether Nietzsche's doctrine of 'eternal recurrence' is a cosmological theory or a myth (somewhat like Plato's Gyges'-Ring myth) used for testing one's moral fibre. I see the doctrine primarily as an existential 'test' devised by Nietzsche to assess one's commitment to life. On this subject, see Friedrich Kaulbach, *Nietzsches Idee einer Experimental-Philosophie* (Cologne: Bohlaer, 1980) pp. 174–85; Karl Jaspers, *Nietzsche* (Chicago, Ill.: Regnery, 1966) p. 353; and Harold Alderman, *Nietzsche's Gift* (Athens, Ohio: Ohio University Press, 1977) pp. 83–112.

120. For an interpretation of the social implications of Nietzsche's concept of the superman, see my *The Unbinding of Prometheus* (Long Island, N.Y.: Libra, 1976) ch. III.C.
121. Dewey, *Human Nature and Conduct*, p. 10.
122. *Ibid.*, p. 284.
123. *Ibid.*, p. 328.
124. John Dewey and James Tufts, *Ethics* (New York: Holt, 1926) pp. 363 and 606. Although Dewey does not allow for a purely private morality (see p. 31 above), subjective personal moral growth is both a condition for, and conditioned by, one's contributions to the objective progress of natural and social evolution.
125. Thomas Nagel, *Mortal Questions* (Cambridge: Cambridge University Press, 1979) p. 126.
126. Bruce Ackerman, *Social Justice in the Liberal State* (New Haven, Conn. and London: Yale University Press, 1970) p. 11.
127. Ronald Dworkin, *Talking Rights Seriously* (Cambridge, Mass.: Harvard University Press, 1978; and London: Duckworth, 1981) pp. 275–8.
128. Peter Singer, *Practical Ethics* (Cambridge: Cambridge University Press, 1979) p. 12.
129. See R. M. Hare, *The Language of Morals* (Oxford: Oxford University Press, 1952); and Marcus Singer, *Generalization in Ethics* (New York: Random House, 1961).
130. See John Rawls, *A Theory of Justice* (Cambridge, Mass.: Harvard University Press, 1971; and Oxford: Oxford University Press, 1973); also H. Kainz, *Democracy East and West* (London: Macmillan, and New York: St Martin's Press, 1984) pp. 43–5.
131. See, for example, Raoul Naroll, *The Moral Order: An Introduction to the Human Situation* (Beverly Hills, Cal.: Sage Publications, 1983) p. 47; also R. B. J. Walker, *World Politics and Western Reason: Universalism, Pluralism, Hegemony* (New York: Institute for World Order, 1982); and Richard Falk and Samuel S. Kim, *An Approach to World Order Studies and the World System* (New York: Institute for World Order, 1982).
132. Josiah Royce, *The Problem of Christianity* (Chicago, Ill.: Regnery, 1968).
133. Raphael, *Moral Philosophy*, p. 16.
134. See David Little, 'Calvin and the Prospects for a Christian Theory of Natural Law', in *Norm and Context in Christian Ethics*, ed. Gene Outka and Paul Ramsey (New York: Scribner's, 1968).
135. Pope Paul VI, *Humanae vitae*, para. 11. On difficulties arising from the conjunction of moral and religious argumentation by religious authorities, see my *Wittenburg, Revisited: A Polymorphous Critique of Religion and Theology* (Washington, D.C.: University Press of America, 1981) pp. 18–20; see also p. 123 below.
136. James M. Gustafson, *Protestant and Roman Catholic Ethics: Prospects for Rapprochement* (Chicago, Ill. and London: University of Chicago Press, 1978) pp. 71, 141ff.

## Notes to Chapter 4: Religious Good and the Common Good

1. Discussed in H. Kainz, *Hegel's Phenomenology*, Part I: *Analysis and Commentary* (Tuscaloosa, Ala.: University of Alabama Press, 1976) pp. 123–5.
2. Søren Kierkegaard, *Either/Or*, II, p. 172.
3. See, for example, Ezekiel 36: 23–8; I John 2: 27.
4. For a discussion of the ethical significance of the myth of the 'tree of knowledge of good and evil', see H. Kainz, *Ethica Dialectica*, ch. I.
5. Arnold Toynbee, *A Study of History*, Sommerville abridgement (Oxford: Oxford University Press, 1967) II, ch. 26, 3(a) and 3(d).
6. See especially Pierre Teilhard de Chardin, *Phenomenon of Man*, trs. B. Wall (New York: Harper, 1961) Books III–IV; *The Future of Man*, trs. N. Denny (New York: Harper and Row, 1964) chs 3 and 18–22; and *The Divine Milieu*, trs. B. Wall (New York: Harper, 1960) Part III.
7. See I Corinthians 12: 12–17; Romans 12: 4–5; Colossians 2: 29; Ephesians 4: 16.
8. See H. Kainz, *The Philosophy of Man*, ch. 5.
9. See H. Kainz, 'Pierre Teilhard de Chardin: A Bio-Doctrinal Study', *Way*, vol. XXVII (1972) no. 6, pp. 18–22.
10. On possibilities for economic and/or political modifications in capitalism and communism, see H. Kainz, *Democracy East and West*, p. 95n.

## Notes to Chapter 5: The Fully Differentiated Moral Good

1. John Dewey, *Reconstruction in Philosophy* (New York: Holt, 1920) p. 175.
2. *Ibid.*, p. 176.
3. On Dewey's ethics, see H. Kainz, 'Pragmatism, Pragmatic Ethics, and Reconstructed Philosophy: Some Metaphilosophical Considerations', *Divus Thomas* (Piacenza, Italy) vol. LXXVIII (July 1975) no. 3, pp. 267–70.
4. See p. 107.
5. See above, pp. 54–7.
6. Kant, *Fundamental Principles of the Metaphysic of Morals*, p. 47n.
7. Thomas R. Flynn, *Sartre and Marxist Existentialism* (Chicago, Ill. and London: University of Chicago Press, 1984) pp. 179, 186.
8. See above, pp. 90–3.
9. Plato, *Apology*, 31D, 40A.
10. Walter Harrelson, *The Ten Commandments and Human Rights* (Philadelphia, Pa.: Fortress Press, 1980) p. 42.
11. Eduard Nielson, *The Ten Commandments in New Perspective* (Chicago, Ill.: Allenson, 1968) pp. 78–86.
12. Harrelson, *The Ten Commandments and Human Rights*, pp. 54–92.
13. *Ibid.*, p. 84.
14. *Ibid.*, p. 142.
15. J. Kovesi, *Moral Notions* (New York: Humanities Press, 1971) ch. 1, sect. 4.

## Notes to Chapter 6: Interconnections

1. See Gilbert Ryle, *The Concept of Mind* (London: Hutchinson, 1949). 'Category mistakes' may be approached on a linguistic level (the level in which Ryle was particularly interested) or on an ontological level (for example, a non-materialist might agree with Ryle not on the basis of linguistic analysis but on the basis of his own thesis about the unique, spiritual nature of mind). In ethics, category mistakes may be considered on the linguistic level (is one using ethical categories consistently?) and/or on the level of first-order values (is one using an ethical category for a matter of aesthetics, a political category for an ethical matter, etc.?).
2. See, for example, Percy Bysshe Shelley's conjectures concerning the moral effect of poetry in his 'A Defence of Poetry'; and, with regard to the effect of aesthetic surroundings on the general moral climate, see A. K. Bierman, *The Philosophy of Urban Existence*, (Athens, Ohio: Ohio University Press, 1973) ch. 14.
3. See Cranston's arguments in H. Kainz, *Ethica Dialectica*, pp. 105–6.
4. See, for example, F. J. Kallmann, 'Twins and Susceptibility to Overt Male Homosexuality', *American Journal of Human Genetics*, vol. IV (1952) pp. 136–46; Sidney Margolese, 'Androsterone/Etiocholanolane Ratios in Male Homosexuals', *Hormones and Behaviour*, vol. I (1970) no. 151, pp. 207–10; and Nanette Gartrell, Lynn Loriaux and Thomas Chase, 'Plasma Testosterone in Homosexual and Heterosexual Women', *American Journal of Psychiatry*, vol. CXXXIV (Oct. 1979) no. 10, pp. 117–18.
5. Susan Griffin, *Pornography and Silence* (New York: Harper and Row, 1981).
6. *Ibid.*, p. 88.
7. Bertrand Russell, *Marriage and Morals* (New York: Liveright, 1929) p. 133.
8. Ch. 3, p. 96.
9. Ch. 4, pp. 98–102.
10. See Genesis XXII; Kierkegaard's famous *Fear and Trembling* is the most eloquent defence of this interpretation.
11. See p. 75.
12. Freud, *Civilization and Its Discontents*, pp. 56–9.
13. Pope Paul VI, *On the Regulation of Birth* (Washington, D.C.: United States Catholic Conference, 1968) p. 13.
14. Raphael, *Moral Philosophy*, p. 57.
15. Quoted by David Shipler in *Russia: Broken Idols, Solemn Dreams* (New York: Times Books, and London: Macdonald, 1983) p. 107.
16. *Ibid.*, p. 110.
17. Karl Marx, *Grundrisse*, section F, in R. Tucker (ed.), *The Marx–Engels Reader* (New York: W. W. Norton, 1978) pp. 276ff.; and *Capital*, I, ch. XXV, section 3.
18. Karl Marx, *The Economic and Philosophic Manuscripts of 1844*, Appendix (Engel's 'Outline of a Critique of Political Economy'), p. 218.

19. See, for example, Julian Simon, *The Economics of Population Growth* (Princeton, N.J.: Princeton University Press, 1977) p. 487.
20. *Ibid.*, p. 491.
21. Cf. Nick Eberstadt, 'Population and Economic Growth', *Wilson Quarterly* x (Winter 1986) no. 5. Eberstadt concludes: 'To assume, as many academics and public officials do, that preventing the birth of poor people will help eliminate poverty appears to be a fundamental error. Mass affluence is the result of human productivity and human organization' (p. 127).
22. On opposing viewpoints in this dispute, see H. Kainz, *Ethica Dialectica*, ch. 6.

# Bibliography

Ackerman, Bruce, *Social Justice in the Liberal State* (New Haven, Conn. and London: Yale University Press, 1970).

Alderman, Harold, *Nietzsche's Gift* (Athens, Ohio: Ohio University Press, 1977).

Allport, Gordon, *Pattern and Growth in Personality* (New York: Holt, Rinehart and Winston, 1961).

Aquinas, Thomas, *Expositio in X lib. Ethicorum ad Nic. Aristotelis*, Parma edition (1852–73) vol. xxi.

——, *Summa theologiae* (Madrid: Biblioteca de Autores Cristianos, 1958).

Aristotle, *Nicomachean Ethics*, trs. W. D. Ross, in *Basic Works of Aristotle*, ed. R. McKeon (New York: Random House, 1941).

——, *Politics*, trs. B. Jowett in *Basic Works of Aristotle*, ed. R. McKeon (New York: Random House, 1941).

Baier, Annette C., 'What Do Women Want in a Moral Theory?', *Nous*, vol. 19 (1985) no. 1.

Baier, Kurt, *The Moral Point of View* (Ithaca, N.Y.: Cornell University Press, 1958).

Beardsley, Monroe, *Aesthetics: Problems in the Philosophy of Criticism* (New York: Harcourt Brace, 1958).

Benedict, Ruth, 'Anthropology and the Abnormal', in *The Philosophy of Society*, ed. R. Beehle (London: Methuen, 1978).

Bentham, Jeremy, *An Introduction to the Principles of Morals and Legislation*, ed. J. H. Burns, James Henderson and H. L. A. Hart (New York: Russell and Russell, and Atheon Press, 1962).

Bierman, A. K., *The Philosophy of Urban Existence* (Athens, Ohio: Ohio University Press, 1973).

Bisbee, Cynthia C., Robert W. Mullaly and Humphry Osmond, 'Temperament and Psychiatric Illness', *Journal of Orthomolecular Psychiatry*, vol. xii (1983) no. 1, pp. 19–25.

Bloch, Ernst, *Natural Law and Human Dignity*, trs. D. Schmidt (Cambridge, Mass. and London: MIT Press, 1986).

Bourke, Vernon J., *The History of Ethics* (Garden City, N.Y.: Doubleday, 1968).

Bradley, F. H., 'My Station and its Duties', in his *Ethical Studies* (Oxford: Clarendon Press, 1927).

Bullough, Edward, '"Psychical Distance" as a Factor in Art and an Aesthetic Principle', in *Aesthetics and the Philosophy of Criticism*, ed. M. Levich (New York: Random House, 1963).

Caplan, Arthur, and Bruce Jennings (eds), *Darwin, Marx and Freud: Their Influence on Moral Theory* (New York and London: Plenum Press, 1954).

Carritt, E. F., *The Theory of Morals* (London: Oxford University Press, 1928).

Chroust, Anton-Hermann, 'The Function of Law and Justice in the Ancient World and the Middle Ages', *Journal of the History of Ideas*, vol. vii (Jan. 1949) no. 1, pp. 298–317.

Colp, Ralph, Jr, 'The Contacts between Karl Marx and Charles Darwin', *Journal of the History of Ideas*, vol. 35 (April/June 1974) no. 2, pp. 329–38.

Deeley, John, and Raymond Nogar, *The Problem of Evolution: A Study of the Philosophical Repercussions of Evolutionary Science* (New York: Appleton-Century-Crofts, 1973).

Dessoir, M., *Aesthetics and Theory of Art* (Detroit, Mich.: Wayne State University Press, 1970).

Dewey, John, *Ethics* (New York: Holt, 1908).

——, *Human Nature and Conduct* (New York: Random House, 1930).

——, *Reconstruction in Philosophy* (New York: Holt, 1920).

——, *Theory of the Moral Life* (New York: Holt, Rinehart and Winston, 1960).

—— and James Tufts, *Ethics* (New York: Holt, 1926).

Donagan, Alan, *Human Ends and Human Actions* (Milwaukee, Wis.: Marquette University Press, 1985).

Doxiadis, Constantinos, 'The Coming World-City: Ecumenopulis', in *Cities of Destiny*, ed. A. Toynbee (New York: Weathervane Books, 1967).

Dworkin, Ronald, *Taking Rights Seriously* (Cambridge, Mass.: Harvard University Press, 1978; and London: Duckworth, 1981).

Ebbinghaus, Julius, 'Interpretation and Misinterpretation of the Categorical Imperative', *Philosophical Quarterly*, vol. iv (April 1954) no. 15, pp. 97–108.

Edwards, Carolyn, 'The Comparative Study of the Development of Moral Judgment and Reasoning', in *Handbook of Cross-Cultural Human Development*, ed. R. Munroe (New York: Garland, 1981).

——, 'Moral Development in Comparative Cultural Perspectives', in *Cultural Perspectives on Child Development*, ed. D. Wagner and H. Stevenson (New York: Freeman, 1982).

Epictetus, *Discourses*, trs. G. Long (Chicago, Ill.: Britannica Great Books, 1952).

——, *The Golden Sayings*, trs. H. Crossley (New York: Collier, 1937) Harvard Classics series.

Eysenck, H. J., *The Biological Basis of Personality* (Springfield, Ill.: Charles C. Thomas, 1967).

——, *Sex and Personality* (Austin, Tx.: University of Texas Press, and West Compton House: Shepton Mallet, Som., 1976).

Falk, Richard and Samuel S. Kim, *An Approach to World Order Studies and the World System* (New York: Institute for World Order, 1982).

Farrell, Patrick, 'Sources of St Thomas' Concept of Natural Law', *The Thomist*, vol. xx (July 1957) no. 3, pp. 249–54.

Fichte, Johann Gottlieb, *The Science of Ethics*, trs. Kroeger (London: Kegan Paul, 1907).

Flanagan, Owen J., Jr, 'Virtue, Sex and Gender: Some Philosophical Reflections on the Moral Psychology Debate', *Ethics*, vol. 92 (April 1982).

Flynn, Thomas R., *Sartre and Marxist Existentialism* (Chicago, Ill. and London: University of Chicago Press, 1984).

Freud, Sigmund, *Civilization and Its Discontents*, trs. James Strachey (New York: W. W. Norton, 1961; London: Hogarth, 1963).

——, *The Ego and the Id*, trs. Joan Riviere (New York: W. W. Norton, 1960).

Fu, Charles Wei-Hsun, 'Marxism–Leninism–Maoism as an Ethical Theory', *Journal of Chinese Philosophy*, vol. 5 (1978) pp. 343–62.

Gartrell, Nanette, Lynn Loriaux and Thomas Chase, 'Plasma Testosterone in Homosexual and Heterosexual Women', *American Journal of Psychiatry*, vol. cxxxiv, 10 (Oct. 1979) pp. 1117–18.

Gauthier, David, 'On the Refutation of Utilitarianism', in *The Limits of Utilitarianism*, eds. Harlan B. Miller and William H. Williamson (Minneapolis, Minn.: University of Minnesota Press, 1982).

Gesell, Arnold and Frances Ilg, *The Child from Five to Ten* (New York and London: Harper, 1946).

Gilligan, Carol, *In a Different Voice: Psychological Theory and Women's Development* (Cambridge, Mass. and London: Harvard University Press, 1982).

——, 'Woman's Place in Man's Life Cycle', *Harvard Educational Review*, vol. 49 (1979) pp. 431–46.

Grant, Michael, *Jesus: An Historian's Review of the Gospels* (New York: Scribner, 1977; London: Sphere, 1978).

Griffin, Susan, *Pornography and Silence* (New York: Harper and Row, 1981).

Grotius, Hugo, *The Law of War and Peace*, trs. L. Loomis (Roslyn, N.Y.: Walter Black, 1949).

Gustafson, James M., *Protestant and Roman Catholic Ethics: Prospects for Rapprochement* (Chicago, Ill. and London: University of Chicago Press, 1978).

Hampshire, Stuart, *Morality and Conflict* (Cambridge, Mass.: Harvard University Press and Oxford: Blackwell, 1983).

Hancock, Roger N., *Twentieth-Century Ethics* (New York and London: Columbia University Press, 1974).

Harding, Arthur L., T. Davitt and R. Wilkin (eds), *Origins of the Natural Law Tradition* (Port Washington, N.Y. and London: Kennikat Press, 1971).

Hare, R. M., *The Language of Morals* (Oxford: Oxford University Press, 1952).

Harrelson, Walter, *The Ten Commandments and Human Rights* (Philadelphia, Pa.: Fortress Press, 1980).

Hegel, G. W. F., *The Philosophy of Mind*, trs. W. Wallace (Oxford: Clarendon Press, 1971).

——, *The Philosophy of Right*, trs. T. M. Knox (Oxford: Oxford University Press, 1967).

Hook, Sidney, *From Hegel to Marx* (Ann Arbor, Mich.: University of Michigan Press, 1962).

Jaspers, Karl, *Nietzsche* (Chicago, Ill.: Regnery, 1966).

Jung, Carl G., *Psychological Types, or The Psychology of Individuation*, trs. H. Godwin Baynes (London: Routledge and Kegan Paul, 1923).

Kainz, Friedrich, *Aesthetics: The Science*, trs. H. Schueller (Detroit, Mich.: Wayne State University Press, 1962).

Kainz, H., *Democracy East and West* (London: Macmillan; New York: St Martin's Press, 1984).

——, *Ethica Dialectica: A Study in Ethical Oppositions* (The Hague: Nijhoff, 1979).

——, *Hegel's Phenomenology*, Part I: *Analysis and Commentary* (Tuscaloosa, Ala.: University of Alabama Press, 1976).

——, *Hegel's 'Philosophy of Right' with Marx's Commentary: A Handbook for Students* (The Hague: Nijhoff, 1974).

——, *The Philosophy of Man: An Introduction to Some Perennial Issues* (Tuscaloosa, Ala.: University of Alabama Press, 1980).

——, *The Unbinding of Prometheus* (Long Island, N.Y.: Libra, 1976).

——, *Wittenburg Revisited: A Polymorphous Critique of Religion and Theology* (Washington, D.C.: University of America Press, 1981).

——, 'Kierkegaard's "Three Stages" and the Levels of Spiritual Maturity', *Modern Schoolman*, vol. LII (1975) no. 4, pp. 368ff.

——, 'Pierre Teilhard de Chardin: A Bio-Doctrinal Study', *Way*, vol. XXVII (1972) no. 6, pp. 18–22.

——, 'Pragmatism, Pragmatic Ethics, and Reconstructed Philosophy: Some Metaphysical Considerations', *Divus Thomas* (Piacenza, Italy) vol. LXXVIII (July 1975) no. 3, pp. 267–70.

Kallmann, F. J., 'Twins and Susceptibility to Overt Male Homosexuality', *American Journal of Human Genetics*, vol. IV (1952) pp. 136–46.

Kant, Immanuel, *Anthropology*, trs. M. Gregor (The Hague: Nijhoff, 1974).

——, *Critique of Practical Reason and Other Works on the Theory of Ethics* (London: Longman, Green, 1909).

——, *The Critique of Pure Reason*, trs. N. K. Smith (New York: St Martin's Press, and London: Macmillan, 1963).

——, *Fundamental Principles of the Metaphysic of Morals*, trs. Thomas K. Abbot (Indianapolis, Ind.: Bobbs-Merrill, 1949).

——, *Ethical Philosophy*, trs. J. Ellington (Indianapolis, Ind.: Hackett, 1983).

——, *On History*, ed. and trs. L. W. Beck (Indianapolis, Ind.: Bobbs-Merrill, 1963).

Kaulbach, Friedrich, *Nietzsches Idee einer Experimental-Philosophie* (Cologne: Bohlaer, 1980).

Kierkegaard, Søren, *The Concept of Dread*, trs. Walter Lowrie (Princeton, N.J.: Princeton University Press, 1957).

——, *Either/Or*, trs. Walter Lowrie (New York: Anchor, 1959).

Klubertanz, George P., *The Discursive Power: Sources and Doctrine of the 'Vis Cogitativa' According to St Thomas Aquinas* (St Louis, Mo.: Modern Schoolman, 1952; printed by The Messenger Press, Carthagena, Ohio).

Kohlberg, Lawrence, 'Education for Justice', in *Moral Education*, ed. J. Sizer (Cambridge, Mass.: Harvard University Press, 1970).

——, *The Psychology of Moral Development* (San Francisco, Cal.: Harper and Row, 1984).

——, C. Levine and A. Hewer, *Moral Stages: A Current Formulation and a Response to Critics* (New York: S. Korger, 1983).

Kovesi, J., *Moral Notions* (London: Routledge and Kegan Paul, 1967; and New York: Humanities Press, 1971).

Lester, David, 'Deviation in Sheldonian Physique-Temperament Match and Neuroticism', *Psychological Reports*, vol. 4 (Dec. 1977), no. 3, p. 942.

Little, David, 'Calvin and the Prospects for a Christian Theory of Natural Law', in *Norm and Context in Christian Ethics*, ed. Gene Outka and Paul Ramsey (New York: Scribner's, 1968).

McLellan, David, *Karl Marx: His Life and Thought* (New York: Harper and Row, 1973).

—— (ed.), *The Marx–Engels Reader* (Oxford: Oxford University Press, 1977).

MacIntyre, Alasdair, *After Virtue: A Study in Moral Theory* (Notre Dame, Ind.: Notre Dame University Press; and London: Duckworth, 1981).

McMurtry, John, *The Structure of Marx's World-View* (Princeton, N.J.: Princeton University Press, 1978).

Macoby, Eleanor, and Carol Jacklin, *The Psychology of Sex Differences* (Stanford, Cal.: Stanford University Press, 1974).

Marcus Aurelius, *Meditations*, trs. G. Long (New York: Collier, 1937) Harvard Classics Series.

Margolese, Sidney, 'Androsterone/Etiocholanolane Ratios in Male Homosexuals', *Hormones and Behavior*, vol. 1 (1970) no. 151, pp. 207–10.

Marx, Karl, *Capital*, vol. 1, trs. B. Fowkes (New York: Vintage, 1977).

——, *Critique of Hegel's Philosophy of Right*, trs. J. O'Malley (Cambridge: Cambridge University Press, 1970).

——, *The Economic and Philosophic Manuscripts of 1844*, trs. Martin Milligan (New York: International Publishers, 1964).

—— and Friedrich Engels, *The Communist Manifesto*, trs. F. Randall (New York: Washington Square Press, 1964).

Midgley, Mary, 'Is "Moral" a Dirty Word?', *Philosophy*, vol. xlvii (July 1972) no. 181, pp. 210ff.

Miller, Richard, *Analyzing Marx: Morality, Power and History* (Princeton, N.J.: Princeton University Press, 1984).

Murphy, J. M., and Carol Gilligan, 'Moral Development in Late Adolescence and Adulthood: A Critique and Reconstruction of Kohlberg's Theory', *Human Development*, vol. 23 (1980).

Nagel, Thomas, *Mortal Questions* (Cambridge: Cambridge University Press, 1979).

Naroll, Raoul, *The Moral Order: An Introduction to the Human Situation* (Beverly Hills, Cal.: Sage Publications, 1983).

Nielson, Eduard, *The Ten Commandments in New Perspective* (Chicago, Ill.: Allenson, 1968).

Nietzsche, Friedrich, *The Will to Power*, trs. W. Kaufmann (New York: Vintage, 1968).

Noddings, Nel, *Caring: A Feminine Approach to Ethics and Moral Education* (Berkeley and Los Angeles, Cal., and London: University of California Press, 1984).

Norman, Richard, *The Moral Philosophers* (Oxford: Clarendon Press, 1983).

Parker, D. H., *The Principles of Aesthetics* (New York: Appleton-Century-Crofts, 1946; and London: Greenwood Press, 1977).

Paton, H. J., *The Categorical Imperative* (London: Hutchinson, 1967).

Paul VI (Pope), *On the Regulation of Birth (Humanae vitae)* (Washington, D.C.: United States Catholic Conference, 1968).

Plato, *Apology*, trs. B. Jowett in *The Dialogues of Plato* (New York: Random House, 1937).

——, *Euthyphro*, trs. B. Jowett (New York: Random House, 1937).

——, *Phaedo*, trs. B. Jowett (New York: Random House, 1937).

——, *The Republic*, trs. B. Jowett (New York: Random House, 1937).

Price, Richard, *A Review of the Principal Questions in Morals* (Oxford: Clarendon Press, 1948).

Ramsey, Paul, *The Truth of Value: A Defense of Moral and Literary Judgement* (Atlantic Highlands, N.J.: Humanities Press, 1985).

Raphael, D. D., *Moral Philosophy* (Oxford: Oxford University Press, 1981).

Rawls, John, *A Theory of Justice* (Cambridge, Mass.: Harvard University Press, 1971; and Oxford: Oxford University Press, 1973).

Rorty, Richard, *Philosophy and the Mirror of Nature* (Oxford: Blackwell, 1980).

Ross, W. D., *The Foundations of Ethics* (Oxford: Clarendon Press, 1939).

Royce, Josiah, *The Problem of Christianity* (Chicago, Ill.: Regnery, 1968).

Rubel, Maximilien, and Margaret Manale, *Marx without Myth* (New York: Harper, 1976).

Russell, Bertrand, *Marriage and Morals* (New York: Liveright, 1929).

Ryle, Gilbert, *The Concept of Mind* (London: Hutchinson, 1949).

Sahlin, Marshall, *The Use and Abuse of Biology* (Ann Arbor, Mich.: University of Michigan Press, 1976).

Sartre, Jean-Paul, *Being and Nothingness*, trs. H. Barnes (New York: Washington Square Press, 1966).

——, 'Existentialism is a Humanism', in *Existentialism*, ed. Walter Kaufmann (New York: Meridian, 1956).

Sheldon, William H., *The Varieties of Temperament* (New York: Harper and Row, 1942).

Shipler, David, *Russia: Broken Idols, Solemn Dreams* (New York: Times Books, and London: Macdonald, 1983).

Sidgwick, Henry, *The Methods of Ethics*, 7th rev. edn (Chicago, Ill.: University of Chicago Press, 1901).

Simon, Julian, *The Economics of Population Growth* (Princeton, N.J.: Princeton University Press, 1977).

Singer, Marcus, *Generalization in Ethics* (New York: Random House, 1961).

——, 'The Categorical Imperative', *The Philosophical Review*, vol. LXIII (Oct. 1954) no. 4, pp. 577–91.

Singer, Peter, *The Expanding Circle: Ethics and Sociobiology* (New York: Farrar, Straus and Giroux; and Oxford: Oxford University Press, 1981).

——, *Practical Ethics* (Cambridge: Cambridge University Press, 1979).

——, 'Ethics and Sociobiology', *Philosophy and Public Affairs*, vol. I (Winter 1982) no. 1.

Smith, Adam, *The Theory of Moral Sentiments* (Oxford: Clarendon Press, 1976).

Spinoza, Benedict, *Ethics*, trs. W. H. White and A. H. Stirling (Oxford: Oxford University Press, 1927).

Stewart, Horace, 'Body Type, Personality, Temperament and Psychotherapeutic Treatment of Female Adolescents', *Adolescence*, vol. 17 (Fall 1982) pp. 621–5.

——, 'Body Type, Personality, Temperament and Psychotherapeutic Treatment of Male Adolescents', *Adolescence*, vol. 15 (Winter 1980) pp. 927–32.

Strassman, Erwin O., 'Physique, Temperament, and Intelligence in Infertile Women', *International Journal of Fertility*, vol. 9 (1964) no. 2.

Sumner, William G., *Folkways* (New York: Ginn, 1907).

Tavris, Carol, and Carole Offir, *The Longest War: Sex Differences in Perspective* (New York: Harcourt Brace Jovanovich, 1977).

Taylor, A. E., *Aristotle* (New York: Dover, 1955).

Taylor, Richard, *Ethics, Faith and Reason* (Englewood Cliffs, N.J.: Prentice-Hall, 1981).

Teilhard de Chardin, Pierre, *The Divine Milieu*, trs. B. Wall (New York: Harper, 1960).

——, *The Future of Man*, trs. N. Denny (New York: Harper and Row, 1964).

——, *Phenomenon of Man*, trs. B. Wall (New York: Harper, 1961).

Telfer, Elizabeth, *Happiness* (New York: St Martin's Press, 1980).

Toynbee, Arnold, *A Study of History*, Sommerville abridgement (Oxford: Oxford University Press, 1967).

Tracy, Theodore, *Physiological Theory and the Doctrine of the Mean in Plato and Aristotle* (Paris: Mouton, 1969).

Tucker, Robert, *Philosophy and Myth in Karl Marx* (Cambridge: Cambridge University Press, 1965).

Veatch, Henry, *For an Ontology of Morals: A Critique of Contemporary Ethical Theory* (Evanston, Ill.: Northwestern University Press, 1971).

——, 'Are There Non-moral Goods?', *The New Scholasticism*, vol. LII (Autumn 1978) no. 4, p. 476.

——, 'The Rational Justification of Moral Principles: Can There Be Such a Thing?', *Review of Metaphysics*, vol. XXXI (Dec. 1977) no. 2, pp. 218–19.

Von Leyden, W., *Aristotle on Equality and Justice* (New York: St Martin's Press, 1985).

Walker, R. B. J., *World Politics and Western Reason: Universalism, Pluralism, Hegemony* (New York: Institute for World Order, 1982).

Willerman, Lee, *The Psychology of Individual and Group Differences* (San Francisco, Cal., and Oxford: W. H. Freeman, 1979).

Wills, Garry, *Inventing America: Jefferson's Declaration of Independence* (New York: Doubleday, 1978; and London: Athlone, 1980).

Wilson, Edward O., *On Human Nature* (Cambridge, Mass.: Harvard University Press, 1978).

——, *Sociobiology: The New Synthesis* (Cambridge, Mass.: Harvard University Press, 1975).

Wilson, James Q., and Richard Herrnstein, *Crime and Human Nature* (New York: Simon and Schuster, 1985).

Wolf, Erik, *Das Problem der Naturrechtslehre: Versuch einer Orientierung* (Karlsruhe: Müller, 1955).

# Index

156